JEWISH JOKES
FOR THE JOHN

DEDICATION

To all the Hymies and the Shlermies,
the Abies and their Beckies,
to the Holtzsteins and the Goldsteins,
and innumerable witz's,
the Gerbers, the Bergers,
the Yettas and the Jakes,
without whom everyone in this book would
   have been named John or Mary,
and a whole complete different title we
   would have needed!

Show me a male and female who've been happy for ten years and I'll show you a Jewish mother and her ten-year-old son.

A woman sat down at the pool of one of Miami Beach's leading hotels. Sitting next to her was an elderly lady wearing the biggest diamond she had ever seen. She turned to the lady and said, "Pardon me, I just can't help admiring the diamond you are wearing. It is the most fantastic I have ever seen."

The little old lady turned to her, smiled, and said, "Thank you. This is the Plotnick Diamond. It is just a carat smaller than the Star of India and is valued even higher than the Hope Diamond. And like those other stones, it too has a curse."

The woman asked, "What **is** the curse of the Plotnick Diamond?"

Sighed the old lady, "Mr. Plotnick."

A Jewish couple found themselves in Florida unable to find a room in a hotel. The only place left to stay in was a hotel that was notorious in its policy of not allowing Jews. The husband turned to his wife and said, "Becky, you keep your big mouth shut, not one word is to come from your lips. Leave it to me, you'll see I'll talk a good English, the man at the desk will never know and we'll get a room."

Sure enough, they walk up to the desk, Dave asks for a room, the hotel desk clerk gives them the key to the room, and they are set. Becky says, "Dave, it's so hot maybe we can go down to the pool for a swim?"

Dave says, "Okay, but, remember not one word is to fall from your mouth." They walk down to the cabanas, Dave signals the cabana boy and he sets up chairs and towels for them.

Becky turns to Dave and asks, "Now can I go into the pool?"

He answers, "Okay, but, remember not a syllable must you utter." Becky goes over to the edge of the pool and sticks one toe into the water, which is icy cold and before she realizes what she is doing, she yells, "Oy vay," whereupon everyone at the pool turns on her. Without blinking an eye she adds, "Whatever that means."

Miami Beach lifeguard to hotel guest: "I've been watching you for the last three days, Mr. Brody, and you'll have to stop urinating in the pool."

Mr. B.: "Everybody urinates in the pool."

Lifeguard: "From the diving board?"

First chorus cutie: "I have a date with that rich clothing manufacturer, Mr. Melnick."

Second cutie: "He's a wolf, he'll tear your dress off."

First cutie: "Thanks for telling me . . . I'll wear an old dress."

The Cohens, married for thirty years, had never missed a night of connubial bliss. Not feeling well one day, the wife consulted her doctor and was informed by the medic that she must have complete rest and quiet for six months.

They decided that they must stay completely apart during this period. She moved into an upstairs bedroom and he remained downstairs.

After three months of complete abstinence and solitude, his will power collapsed and he started for her bedroom. Just as he was about to ascend the stairs, he saw her coming down. Their eyes met and she said, "Dear, I was just coming down to die."

To which he quickly replied, "I'm glad honey, because I was just going up to kill you."

"I'm looking for adventure, excitement, beautiful women," cried Seymour to his father as he prepared to leave home. "Don't try to stop me, I'm on my way!"

"Who's trying to stop you?" shouted his father. "I'll go with you!"

They were unveiling a statue of the Unknown Soldier in Israel. The canvas was pulled off and on the statue was a plaque reading, "Goldberg". One of the men in the audience walked up to the official-in-charge and said, "I thought this statue was for the Unknown Soldier, but there's a name on it, 'Goldberg'."

The official explained, "It's all very simple. As a furrier, Goldberg was the best known man in Israel. But as a soldier, he was completely unknown."

Arthur and Stanley went on a safari. As they were walking through the dark jungle Arthur felt something on his back. He shouted to Stanley, "Tell me quick, is there a leopard on my back?"

Stanley replied, "How would I know, am I a furrier?"

Did you hear about the rabbi who doubled as press agent? He saved his own clippings.

Mr. and Mrs. Goldberg had scrimped and saved to put their eldest son through college. At last, they had the money and decided to send him to a fine high-brow Eastern boarding school. They saw him off on the train, and tearfully bade him farewell.

A few months later, he returned home for the Christmas holidays. The parents were overjoyed to have their son Sammy back with them. The mother greeted him with: "Samelah, oh, it's so good to see you."

"Mother," he replied, "stop calling me Samelah, after all, I'm a grown man now, and I do wish you would refer to me as Samuel."

She apologized and asked, "I hope you only ate Kosher foods while you were away?"

"Mother, we're living in a modern age, and it's preposterous to hang on to old world traditions. I indulged in all types of food, Kosher and non-Kosher, and believe me, you would be better off if you did."

"Well, tell me, did you at least go to the synagogue to offer a prayer of thanks occasionally?"

The son replied: "Really, do you honestly feel going to a synagogue when you're associating with a large percentage of non-Jews is the proper thing to do? Honestly Mother, it's unfair to ask it of me really."

At this point Mrs. Goldberg, fighting back anger, looked at her eldest son and said, "Tell me, Samuel, are you still circumsized?"

An old lady, who was walking her dog, decided to go into the local supermarket, which didn't allow dogs. She tied the animal to a fire hydrant. No sooner was the dog tied when every dog in the neighborhood that was loose started sniffing this defenseless animal. The cop on the corner, observing what was happening, called to the old woman and told her that she couldn't leave her dog there alone.

She asked him why and he replied, "Lady, your dog is in heat."

She answered, "Eat, she'll eat anything."

He countered, "The dog should be bred."

The old lady replied, "She'll eat bread, cake, anything you give her she'll eat."

In complete frustration he said, "That dog should be laid!"

The old woman stared directly into his eyes and answered, "So lay her. I always wanted a police dog."

A guy walked into a clothing store and said, "Hey, Harry, I was sorry to hear about your fire."

Harry quickly replied, "Shhh, the fire's not till tomorrow."

An Israeli soldier went to his commanding officer and asked for a weekend pass. "A weekend pass? But you've only been in the army twelve days," the commanding officer said. The soldier pleaded until the commanding officer relented. "If you want a weekend pass that badly, capture an Egyptian tank and I'll give you one."

The soldier left and returned an hour later with an Egyptian tank.

"How in blazes did you do that?" asked the officer.

"It was easy," said the soldier. "All I did was go out in the desert. When I saw an Egyptian tank I hollered, 'Hey you! Want a weekend pass?' He said, 'Yeah!' So we exchanged tanks."

To his son, the well-known physician, old Jake Speigel continued to complain of severe pains in his left leg. His son tried various treatments and medication but the pain persisted. The old man was becoming impatient. "My son," the old man said, in desperation, "You're a doctor. There must be something you can do for the pain in my leg!"

"Sit down, papa. Listen to me," said the son. "Even doctors have their limitations. You must understand that, with advancing age, certain deterioration takes place. Please try to remember that your leg is eighty-four years old!"

"I'll try to remember," said the old man. "However, I would like to know one thing. Is my other leg maybe ten years younger?"

Walking jaunty jolly along East Broadway, Cantor Leibowitz, wearing his fine black coat with Persian lamb collar, and black homburg, was humming under his breath. "Hmmmmmmmmmmmmmmmmm."

All of a sudden, he heard someone yelling, "Cantor Leibowitz! Cantor Leibowitz!"

He turned and there was a little ragged man who seemed to be coming towards him but he continued on his way for he couldn't imagine that he could be calling to him.

Again he heard, "Cantor Leibowitz! Cantor Leibowitz!" and he felt someone tugging on his coat.

He turned and looked down at the little man. "How do you know I am Cantor Leibowitz?"

"I hear you chant every Saturday morning in the synagogue on Rivington Street!"

"That's very nice." remarked the Cantor and continued walking, humming "Hmm."

Again he heard, "Cantor Leibowitz! Cantor Leibowitz! Your house is on fire!"

"How do you know it's my house?" asked Cantor Leibowitz.

"You live at 302 Eldridge Street, don't you?"

"Yes," replied the Cantor.

"Well," persisted the little man, "Your house is on fire!"

The Cantor removed his tuning fork from his breast pocket, with great flourish, tapped the lamp post and sang out lustily: "Oyyyyyyyyyy! Gevaaaaaaaalt!"

A train in Arizona was boarded by robbers, who went through the pockets of the luckless passengers. One of them happened to be a traveling salesman from New York, who, when his turn came, fished out $200, but rapidly took $4 from the pile and placed it in his vest pocket.

"What do you mean by that?" asked the robber, as he toyed with his revolver.

Hurriedly came the answer: "You surely would not refuse me two per cent discount on a strictly cash transaction like this?"

Why do Jews have big noses? Because the air is free.

"You admit having broken into the same dress shop four times. What did you steal?"

"A dress for my wife, but she made me change it three times."

Martha was dying. With her last breath she turned to Abe and asked, "Abe, before I die, make love to me just one more time."

Abe answered, "How could you ask me to do such a thing, it will kill you."

Martha pleaded, "Everyone is entitled to one last request before they die, you should grant me this last wish."

Abe replied, "Okay." He got into bed and made love to her. No sooner did he finish than she hopped out of bed completely cured, and ran downstairs and started to flick a chicken and yell into the living room where her children were sitting that dinner would be ready in an hour.

The children were astounded and ran up the stairs to their father who was sitting in a chair and crying. They said, "Papa, why are you crying? It's a miracle! Mama is completely cured!"

He replied, "I know, but when I think what I could have done for Eleanor Roosevelt."

A wrench is a Jewish resort with horses.

A Jew exclaimed to his partner at the club: "Great heavens! I came away and left the safe open."

"What does it matter?" said his partner. "Aren't we both here?"

An efficiency expert died and was carried to his grave by six pallbearers. As they approached their destination the lid popped open and the efficiency man sat up and shouted, "If you'd put this thing on wheels, we could lay off four men!"

The toilet seat in the Rabinowitz home was chipped. On his day off, Sidney promised to paint it. He had some nice, bright green enamel in the garage and applied a fresh shiny coat.

Ethel went in with a magazine, sat down to meditate and read. When she tried to get up, she found she was stuck! She yelled for Sid.

He tugged and tugged but could not pry her loose. Ethel, in desperation cried, "So what are you standing there! Call me a doctor! If plaster gets stuck, he at least knows how to remove it without tearing off the skin!"

Sidney dashed to the telephone and pleaded with the doctor to come right over. This was a real emergency! The doctor explained that he had an office full of patients and that he couldn't possibly get there for at least two hours.

Sid had a bright idea. He'd unscrew the hinges and she could lie on the bed on her stomach and wait for the doctor. The two hours seemed like four but the doctor finally arrived.

Sidney directed him into the bedroom and pointing to his wife said, "Doc! Ain't that something? What d'ya think of that?"

The doctor looked thoughtfully and declared, "Very nice...but why such a cheap frame?"

In Israel, a little boy boarded a crowded bus where he had to stand with nothing to hang on to. He reached up and held the beard of an old man near him. After riding this way for a half hour the gentleman said to him, "Look, son, you will have to let go." Whereupon the boy in astonishment replied, "What's the matter—are you getting off here?"

"You don't speak nicely to me the way you used to," Mrs. Zachariah said. "I suppose you just don't love me any more."
"Don't love you," growled her husband. "There you go again! Don't love you! Why, I love you more than life itself. Now shut up and let me read my newspaper."

One of Sol's salesmen died suddenly. Even though the man had worked for him only a short time, he felt that the right thing to do was to visit the widow and offer his condolences. He went to the apartment house where the widow lived and saw a group of men in the elevator. Without thinking twice he followed them and entered an apartment where he saw several more men seated in the living room, not speaking. Every few minutes one of the men would go into an adjoining room, and after a while come out, put on his hat and coat, and leave. He thought to himself, the poor woman must be very bereaved. Suddenly he looked up and a woman beckoned to him from the doorway and ushered him into a darkened bedroom. Before he could stop her, she undressed him, took him to bed and made love to him. After they were finished, he dressed and she walked him to the door. He turned to her and said, "Next time I hope we meet under happier circumstances."

Wife (to seasick husband)—"Look, Jake, over there. Such a big ship!"
Husband—"I don't want to see any ships. Call me when you see a bus."

Sam's so stingy he heats the knives so his wife won't use too much butter.

As he lay on his deathbed he spoke, "Sara, I want you should know before I die that Ginsburg the tailor owes me $200, and Morris the butcher owes me $50, and Klein next door owes me $300." His wife turned to the children and said, "What a wonderful man your father is. Even when he's dying he's got the brains to realize who owes him money." The old man continued, "And Sara I want you to also know that I owe the landlord a hundred dollars." To which his wife cried, "Ho ho, now he's getting delirious!"

I was driving along and I saw this sign that said "Motel" and under it "TV". I stopped at the place, got a room, and found there was no TV set. I told the manager, "There's a sign outside that says TV." The manager said, "Yeah, Tourists Velcome."

Artie Kaplan got his medal during the war for saving two women . . . one for himself and one for the General.

The papa mink says to the mama mink, "If I have a good year, I promise I'll give you a full-length Jew!"

Harry and Tillie were celebrating their 50th wedding anniversary and invited their three sons, their wives and grandchildren to join them for a party. The oldest son stood up and proposed a toast to his parents. He said, "Mom and Dad, I want you to know that no matter what I could think of to give you as a gift I really couldn't think of anything good enough to give parents as wonderful as you."

The middle son stood up and said, "Mom and Dad, I hope you understand why I didn't bring you a present to celebrate this occasion, but, I'm sure you understand that we are in the midst of refurnishing our new summer home and we just couldn't find the time."

The third son, smiling, said, "Mom and Dad, I'm sure you know how much I love you; bringing you a present wouldn't show how sincere I am in my emotions."

The father then stood up and turned to his sons and said, "My dear children, now that Mother and I have celebrated 50 years of living together, I feel it's time to tell you something. You know, when Mother and I met, I was poor, she was poor, I didn't have a job, we didn't even know where our next meal was coming from. Would you believe it, we didn't even have enough money to buy a marriage license."

The oldest son stood up enraged and asked, "Are you trying to tell us that we are bastards?"

The father smiled and answered, "Yes, and cheap ones too!"

He was complaining to his friend that he was losing his manhood. The friend suggested that he try eating rye bread every day. He ran into a bakery and ordered $20.00 worth of poppy seed rye. The baker said: "Twenty dollars worth? Why, it'll get hard before you eat it!"

"In that case," he cried, "give me fifty dollars worth!"

"Will you please explain me the difference between shillings and pence?"
"You can walk down the street without shillings."

Jake came home and found his wife in bed with a stranger.
"What are you two doing?" he screamed.
"See?" said the wife, "I told you he's stupid!"

An old sexton asked his priest, "Father, weren't the Apostles Jews?" He said they were.
Puzzled, the sexton demanded: "Then how the deuce did the Jews let go of a good thing like the Catholic Church and let the Eytalians grab it?"

The local rabbi decided that he had better look into reports of the "fast-life" of the Scarsdale younger set, so he arranged to have himself invited to a week-end house party. Nothing unusual occurred and about midnight he said goodnight and left the youngsters together.

About an hour later, there was a knock on the door that got him out of bed. He opened the door and there stood one of the young lady guests in the flimsiest of nighties, smiling up at him. Assuming a mistake had been made, he said, "Do you want me?"

"Heavens, no!" she chirped. "I drew you."

Television shows are getting longer and longer. Next season, we get a three hour medical epic. They circumsize the Jolly Green Giant.

What happened when the Ajax white knight came to a Jewish neighborhood?
He bought a new suit of armor wholesale.

A woman had some "female trouble" and so she went to see her nephew, who was a gynecologist. After the examination was over she looked him straight in the eye and said, "Tell me, your mother knows how you make a living?"

Mr. Goldberg came home from the office unexpectedly and found his wife in bed with Mr. Cohen, the next door neighbor. Distraught and angry he ran next door and confronted Mrs. Cohen. "Mrs. Cohen," he cried, "your husband is in bed with my wife!"

"Calm down, calm down," Mrs. Cohen said. "Look, don't take it so hard. Sit down, have a glass tea. Relax." Mr. Goldberg sat quietly and drank his tea. It was then he noticed a little glint in Mrs. Cohen's eye. Coyly she suggested, "You want a little revenge?" And with that they withdrew to the couch and made love.

Then they had another glass tea. Then a little more revenge, a little more tea, more revenge, more tea. Finally, Mrs. Cohen looked at Mr. Goldberg and asked, "How about another revenge?"

"I'll tell you, Mrs. Cohen," said Mr. Goldberg quietly, "to be truthful, I ain't got no hard feelings left."

Dr. Adelman's patient was complaining: "Doctor, my memory is very, very faulty. I seem to forget everything. What can I do?" The doctor replied, "Well, the first thing, pay me in advance."

Old man Ginsburg was disgusted with his family. He told his family he was leaving them and going to Japan. The boys asked, "Papa, how will you get there?" He said, "Don't worry, I'll row there."

They walked him to the dock and without their father seeing, tied a very long rope to his row boat. He bid them all farewell and started rowing towards the horizon. They let him stay in the boat all night, but, when the sun began to rise they became nervous about his well-being. There was a tremendous fog and the old man and the boat were not visible. The old man had been rowing away all night when suddenly he heard a voice in the distance shouting, "Abe Ginsburg, are you all right?"

He turned towards the voice and shouted, "Who knows me in Japan?"

A man was seated in a restaurant and ordered a bowl of chicken soup. The waiter brought the soup and walked away quickly. The man studied the soup for a few minutes and demanded to see his waiter. The waiter came back and the customer shouted, "Waiter, taste the soup." The waiter said, "I don't have to taste it, I ate some for lunch and it was delicious." The customer answered, "I insist. Taste the soup." The waiter looked down and saw that he had neglected to give the customer a spoon. He said, "Wait a minute, I'll get a spoon." To which the customer shouted, "Aha!"

Irving Kramer, a leading dress manufacturer, decided to go on an African safari. After spending six weeks in darkest Africa he returned to Seventh Avenue. Everyone who worked in his showroom gasped when he walked in the door. Irving, who was six feet tall when he left New York, was now little higher than two feet. His employees all looked at him and asked, "Mr. Kramer, what happened?"

He replied, "Never, but never, under any circumstances, call a witch doctor a schmuck."

Levi—"What makes you look so sorrowful, Jake?"

Cohen—"I just now sold a two dollar coat to an Irishman for six dollars, and he didn't try to knock me down; I'm kicking myself because I didn't ask ten."

Spokesman of Creditors—"Well, Cohen, we've decide to accept five cents on a dollar —cash."

Cohen, the debtor—"Cash, you say? Then, of course, I get the regular cash discount."

An Israeli sat down in a train between two Arabs. He nodded in a friendly manner, but the Arabs sat in stony silence. The Israeli noticed an Egyptian newspaper on the opposite seat and reached for it. Being a literate man, he was able to decipher much on the printed page. All of a sudden, he turned to the Arab on his right and said, "You look like an intelligent man. I have come upon a word that I cannot quite make out. Would you be good enough to tell me what it is?"

The Arab winked to the other Arab and said, "The word is 'syphilis'!"

The Jew thanked him effusively and read on. A few minutes later, he was again stumped by a word. Turning to the other Arab, he said, "You too are obviously a man of education. Would you kindly tell me what this word is?"

The Arab smirked, scarcely looked at the page, winked at the other Arab and replied, "The word is 'gonorrhea'!"

"Syphilis AND gonorrhea!" was the Israeli's rejoinder. "Oh, that poor Nasser!"

What would you call the first Jewish astronaut that they send to the moon?
Schmuck.

The old father was dying and his family was gathered around the bed waiting for him to take his last breath. As the old man wheezed away life, his oldest son said to one and all, "When Papa goes, if it's tonight, we can bury him early tomorrow from the big funeral parlor downtown. Since the funeral will be early in the morning, we won't be able to get in touch with too many people, so we won't need a lot of cars, or the big room, and it won't cost too much."

His daughter was standing there and she said to the brother, "You know, death to me is very personal. Why do we have to call a bunch of strangers together to witness such a sad scene—if you two boys are there and I'm there who needs anyone else?"

The youngest son looked at them both and said, "I couldn't agree with you more. In fact, why do we need the expense of taking Papa to an undertaker? He is dying in the house, let's bury him from the house."

All of a sudden, the old man's eyes flew wide open. He looked at his three children and shouted, "Give me my pants!"

They answered in a chorus, "Papa, you are a very sick man. Where do you want to go?"

He replied, "Give me my pants. I'll walk to the cemetery."

Ethel and Mollie, who hadn't seen each other for a few months, decided to meet for lunch. Mollie looked at Ethel and said, "Ethel, to tell you the truth, I've never seen you look so good."

Ethel answered, "Mollie, don't tell anyone, but I'm having an affair."

Mollie clapped her hands with glee and asked, "Where?"

Jerry Holtzman went to his tailor to order a suit. After being measured and picking the swatch he desired and giving full details on how he wanted the suit made, he asked the tailor when he would have it ready.

The little tailor replied, "Jerry, the cloth you picked is woven by monks in a monastery high in the Tibetan mountains. It takes six weeks for an expedition to reach them in order to get the cloth. The buttons are made from buffaloes. Just to get three buttons that match is a process that takes four to five weeks. To sew the suit together the way you want takes six Italians, who sit cross-legged for two weeks, sewing each stitch."

Jerry answered, "Listen, I'm all choked up, but you still didn't answer when I can expect delivery."

The tailor thought for a moment and asked, "How's Thursday?"

What's the definition of a Nymphomaniac? A Jewish girl who will go to bed with a guy after she's just had her hair done.

Goldfarb walked into the Fifth Avenue deli-catessen and, pointing to a piece of meat in the showcase, asked: "Give me a pound of that, please."

"You mean that ham?" asked the clerk.

Goldfarb shrieked, "Did I ask you what it was?"

A housemaid had been working for her employer for two years. One day she said, "Mrs. Cohen, I'm pregnant and having no husband, I don't know what to do."

Her employer, being a kindly woman, said, "Don't worry dear, have the child and I will adopt it."

A year and a half went by and the maid approached her employer, saying, "Mrs. Cohen, I'm with child again."

Her employer was annoyed but didn't want to lose the girl's services, so she adopted the second child. too.

Three months after the birth of the second baby, the maid came to the woman and said, "I'm sorry, Mrs. Cohen, but I must leave. I couldn't possibly work for a woman with two children."

A rich manufacturer from New York suffered a nervous breakdown. "You must have a rest," advised his doctor. "Go to Florida. Lay around under the sun, go swimming. You'll be better in a month."

The businessman followed the doctor's advice and went to Miami, got into his swimming shorts and strolled the warm, sandy beach. Then the water was too much to resist and he went for a dip. But he had overestimated all the years he'd gone without exercise and before he realized it he was over his depth and couldn't swim back.

"Help-help!" yelled the businessman. "Save me, I'm drowning."

An alert lifeguard heard the cry, dove into the water, and towed him to safety.

The manufacturer's wife came running to the scene on the beach. "Irving, baby, are you all right? Speak to me..."

"I'm all right," wheezed Irving, dripping water, "but I've got to ask you something in private, please. Bend down."

The worried wife stooped over. "Yes, Irving. What is it that you want to ask me?"

"Tell me, how much do I tip for a thing like this?"

Do you know what they call a Jewish baby that's not circumcised? A girl.

While waiting for the speaker at a public meeting, a little Jew in the audience seemed very nervous. He glanced over his shoulder from time to time and shifted about in his seat. At last he arose and demanded in a high, penetrating voice, "Is there a Christian Scientist in the audience?"

A dignified woman at the other side of the hall rose to her feet and said: "I'm a Christian Scientist."

"Well, then, lady," requested the little Jew, "would you mind changing seats with me? I'm sitting in a draft."

The family managed to bring the patriarchal grandfather from Hungary and he came to live with his daughter and her family. The old man was fascinated by New York and all it had to offer. One day, his grandson Yankel took him to the zoo in Central Park. Most of the animals were familiar to the old man. However, they came to the cage where the laughing hyena was confined, and the old man became curious. "Yankel, in the old country, I never heard of an animal that laughed."

Yankel noticed the keeper standing nearby and approached him.

"My grandfather recently came here from Europe. He says they don't have laughing hyenas there. Could you tell me something about him so that I can, in turn, tell him about it?"

The keeper said, "Well, he eats once a day."

Yankel turned to his grandfather and, in Yiddish, translated, "Zayda, he eats once a day."

The keeper continued, "He takes a bath once a week."

"Zayda, he bathes once a week."

The old man listened intently.

The keeper added, "He mates once a year."

"Zayda, he mates once a year."

The old man shook his head up and down and said thoughtfully, "All right, he eats once a day. He bathes once a week. But if he mates only once a year, why is he laughing?"

MAN: This may be a small diamond but it hasn't one rough flaw.
GIRL: In that diamond there's no room for a flaw.

Teacher—(to class)—"Now children, I want you to write your names in your primers."
Little Abie—"What! And kill the resale value!"

A gentleman visited a Jewish restaurant and was served by a Chinese waiter who made suggestions and took the final order, all in Jewish. After dinner the man called for the proprietor. "Tell me," said the diner, "Isn't it extraordinary that you have a Chinese waiter that speaks Jewish?"

"Shhh," replied the restaurateur. "He thinks we are teaching him English."

A young Jewish couple were being wed in the usual Jewish tradition, surrounded by at least two hundred relatives and friends. The room was in a complete hush as the rabbi reached the part of the service which said, "With all my worldly goods I thee endow." The best man turned to the maid of honor and said, "There goes Irving's bicycle."

A sixty-year-old and an eighty-year-old met. The sixty-year-old said, "I don't know. I just can't seem to satisfy my wife. I try, but— nothing."

The eighty-year-old answered, "I have no problem whatsoever. Every night I come home and I get undressed in front of my wife, and I say 'Take a look. Are you satisfied?' She shrugs 'yes' and that's it."

A family with a son about to be Bar Mitz-
vahed wanted to celebrate the occasion in a
unique way. Money was no object. The caterer suggested many things... flying the party
out to Disneyland, renting out the White
House, having the affair in a nuclear sub-
marine. All of these ideas were rejected by
the family as old hat. It wasn't until the
caterer came up with the idea of having the
Bar Mitzvah on safari in Africa that the
family grew excited. Invitations were issued
to 200 guests, 200 plane tickets were
bought and the group set off for Africa. In
Africa the Bar Mitzvah party was met by 200
elephants, 50 guides, 7 buglers, and 300
native porters who were to carry the food.
Each guest mounted his own elephant with
the father of the Bar Mitzvah boy in the rear
of the procession. They were only several
miles into the jungle when the whole caravan
came to a sudden halt.

From the rear elephant the father cried,
"What's going on here?" And the question
was repeated 200 times till it reached the
head guide at the front of the procession.
The answer came back up the line, "We have
to stop here for a little while." "Why?"
wailed the distressed father; "Why?" wailed
the man in front of him. "Why?" wailed the
200 guests as the question proceeded up
the line.

There was a short pause and then the voice of the chief guide was heard: "There's another Bar Mitzvah ahead of us."

Mr. and Mrs. Jacobs were the bitterest of enemies, and the husband, for an anniversary gift, presented his spouse with a tombstone. On it had been engraved, "Here lies my wife, cold as usual."
In retaliation, wifey went and bought one for him. Her selection read, "Here lies my husband, stiff at last."

A little old Jewish lady sits down on a plane next to a big Norwegian. She keeps staring and staring at him. Finally she turns to him and says, "Pardon me, are you Jewish?"
He replies, "No."
A few minutes go by and she looks at him again and asks, "You can tell me—you are Jewish, aren't you?"
He answers, "Definitely not."
She keeps studying him and says again, "I can tell you are Jewish."
In order to get her to stop annoying him, the gentleman replies, "Okay, I'm Jewish."
She looks at him and shakes her head back and forth, and says, "You don't look it."

A garment manufacturer took his secretary on a buying trip. They got adjoining rooms and retired for the night. About two hours had elapsed when the secretary tiptoed into her boss's room and whispered, "Mr. Grenfeld, would you mind if I stayed here with you?"

"Go ahead," he said. "Make yourself comfortable."

She sat on the couch for a few minutes and then asked, "Mr. Grenfeld, may I get into bed with you?"

"Sure, make yourself comfortable," he replied and fell fast asleep.

His secretary wiggled suggestively a few times but getting no response, poked him in the back. "I'm very thirsty, Mr. Grenfeld," she whispered. "Would you get me a glass of water?"

He looked at her and said, "Tell me my dear, would you like to be Mrs. Grenfeld tonight?"

"Oh," she cooed. "I certainly would!"

"Well," he replied, "then get up and get your own water."

It was their honeymoon night and the Jewish bride had put on a sheer nightgown and crawled into bed . . . only to discover that her Episcopalian husband was about to go to sleep on the couch.

"George," she called out, "aren't you going to make love to me?"

"I can't, honey," he replied, "because it's Lent."

"Why that's awful," she exclaimed, bursting into tears. "To whom, and for how long?"

The clothing salesman had taken an order from a customer for a suit without taking a deposit. It was a rather oversized suit, of an atrocious color. Well, the suit was fixed, but the man never picked up the garment. The boss advised him if that suit wasn't sold within a week, he was going to fire him.

This one day, the boss went out for lunch, and into the store came a blind man with a seeing-eye dog. Right then and there, the salesman decided this was his opportunity to get rid of the suit. Sure enough, he sold it to the man. But an hour later, the boss returned, here was the salesman in a corner, bloody and quite beaten up.

The boss said, "What happened?"

He said, "Well, I sold that suit."

He says, "That's fine. But why are you in this condition?"

"I sold it to a blind man," the salesman replied.

"Well, so what?" the boss asked, "why are you in that condition—all bloody and beaten up?"

The salesman sighed, "After he paid, the seeing-eye dog kicked the hell out of me."

Jake went to his family doctor and in the strictest of confidence asked him the meaning of the word sodomy. The doctor said, "Sodomy is having sex with a cow."

Jake replied, "I can understand that, farm hands far from the city get desperate."

The doctor then added, "Sodomy is having sex with a horse."

Jake replied, "This too I can understand."

The doctor said, "Sodomy is having sex with a dog."

Jake said, "If you can't find a cow or a horse, what else can you do?"

The doctor continued, "Sodomy is having sex with a chicken."

Jake replied, "A chicken! Feh!"

Sadie was dying. She turned to her husband and said, "You haven't spoken to my mother in twenty years. I know I'm dying. My one wish is that when I die you ride in the car behind the hearse with my mother."

Her husband answered, "Okay, but it'll ruin my whole day."

How can you tell a plain Jewish girl from a plain gentile girl?
By her fixed nose, capped teeth, false eyelashes, padded bra and blonde wig.

A timid, rather elderly man employed in the local pickle factory had for years the driving urge to insert his finger in a pickle slicer. One day he returned home early from work all happy and elated, and quite naturally his wife asked him what was the matter.
"Well, doggone it! I done it... I finally went and done it!" said the man.
"What did you do, for Heaven's sake?" asked the wondering wife.
"Put my finger in a pickle slicer! That's what I did, damn it!" blurted out the elderly guy.
"Well, then," asked the wife, "what did they do to you for doing it?"
"Aw!" replied the man, "they fired me, that's what they done."
"And what about the pickle slicer, may I ask?" queried the wife.
"Oh," grinned the husband, "they fired her too!"

Definition of a genius—average student with Jewish parents.

There was this husband who came home to find his wife standing in front of a mirror fondling her breasts. The husband looked at her and said, "What's going on?"
The wife answered, "I just returned from Doctor Silverman and he told me I had the most beautiful breasts he'd ever seen."
The husband looked at her again and said, "Did he say anything about your dead ass?"
She replied, "Your name never came up in the conversation."

Three prosperous but aging industrialists were sunning themselves in the patio of one of Miami Beach's most expensive hotels. "Now that we can afford it, it's hard to enjoy it," one of them said. "Here I am in this beautiful place with all these gorgeous women around and my eyesight is so bad I can hardly make out the surroundings."

"I know," said the second. "It's my stomach that's failing me. I could order lobster, but I have to eat spinach. I love champagne, but I must drink milk."

"Yes," the third man agreed. "I've got a problem, too. Just last night I asked my wife to roll over and she said, 'What! Not again, Harry. We just finished the third one fifteen minutes ago.' You see, with me it's memory."

A little Jew sat down next to a big Texan on a plane. The plane hit rough weather and the Texan fell asleep. The little Jew became violently ill and threw up all over the Texan. The Texan woke up, looked at himself all covered with vomit and the little Jew looked at him, shook his head and asked, "Do you feel better now?"

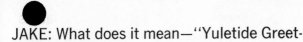

JAKE: What does it mean—"Yuletide Greet-
ings?"
SAM: Lend me $5—you'll tide me over for
a few days.

A Jew and an Irishman were fishing in sepa-
rate boats some distance apart. The Irishman got a bite and was so nervous that he
fell out of the boat. He sank twice and as he
was coming up the second time, the Jew
rowed over and called out:
"Mister, can I have your boat if you don't
come up again?"

As they sank down on the grass at the posh
Catskill resort, he murmered, "I love you."
"But we just now met," she protested.
"I know," he answered. "But I'm only here
for the week-end."

Mrs. Cohen lived in the 30th floor pent-
house of her building. Every day when she
went down in the elevator and up in the elevator the elevator man would see her genu-
flect. After watching this for several days he
couldn't resist asking her if she was Catholic. She replied, "Definitely not, I'm Jewish."
He asked, "I don't understand. If you are
Jewish why do you cross yourself every
time you get in and out of my elevator?"
She answered, "Cross myself! I'm checking
to see if I have my tiara, my brooch, my clip,
. . . MY CLIP!!!

Little Sammy Greenstein from the Bronx, in New York City, had graduated from high school. Papa Greenstein was very proud and told his son: "Sammy-boy, you've done fine in school, and now I'd like you to go to college. Where would you like to attend?"

"I'd like to go to Notre Dame," answered Sammy.

"Notre Dame!" exclaimed the father, "why that's a Catholic college, son."

"Well, pops, a lot of my high school buddies are going there, besides that, they have a great football team. I think I would like it there."

Three and a half years pass and one day Sammy received a telegram from his father: "Dear Son: Yom Kippur tomorrow. Best wishes, Your Dad."

An answer came back within an hour: "Dear Dad: Thanks a lot! I'll put five dollars on him, and say three Hail Mary's to win."

Here's a new drink—Manischewitz and Geritol. It's called a bloody Mendel.

There was a Jewish farmer who had two chickens. One chicken got very sick and, so, he decided to use the best Jewish cure in the world. He killed the healthy chicken to make soup for the sick chicken.

Cohen and Goldberg were partners for many years. One day Cohen came in and told Goldberg that he had changed his name to Carson. The firm then became known as Carson and Goldberg. Several months later Goldberg came into the office and told his partner that he too had changed his name to Carson and the firm became known as Carson and Carson. A buyer called to talk to Mr. Carson, and the switchboard operator queried, "Which one? Goldberg or Cohen?"

The beautiful girl staying in a Miami Beach hotel got out of bed, put a housecoat on over her sheer nightgown, went to her dressing table and began to comb her hair. In the reflection of her mirror, she noticed the window washer cleaning the windows. She decided that she would give him a thrill so she stood up and stretched her arms above her head, looking at him languidly; but he kept on cleaning the windows. She took off her housecoat, stood in her sheer nightie, walked a couple of feet closer to the window, made a few moves with her hips but no reaction came from the window washer. Finally she took off her nightgown, stood there completely nude, walked right up to the window and glared.

The man flung open the window and said, "Wassamatta lady, ain't you ever seen a window washer before?"

Jake came home in the middle of the afternoon. He was met at the door by his wife and his son. His son exclaimed, "Dad, there's a boogey man in the closet."

Jake rushed to the closet and flung the door open. There, huddled among the coats, was his partner, Sam.

"Sam!" shrieked Jake, "why in hell do you come here in the afternoon and scare my kid?"

"Sam," his dying partner wheezed. "I have a confession to make. I robbed our firm of $100,000. I sold the secret formula to our competitors. I took the letter from your desk that your wife needed to get her divorce. And Sam, I ..."

"That's all right, old man. It was me that poisoned you!"

Jack and Al were partners. Every morning Al would walk right into Jack's office and start discussing business. One day Jack looked at Al and said, "Al, you never ask me how I am, how's my family—all you ever talk about is business."

Al said, "Jack, when you're right, you're right. How are you?"

Jack replied, "Don't ask!"

An Englishman and a Jewish friend, talking about conscription, were recalling the war. "And did you join the Army, Abie?" asked the Englishman.
"Yes."
"Serve in France?"
"Yes, three years."
"Did you get a commission?"
"No, just my wages."

The partners agreed that whichever died first was to have $5000 put in his coffin by the other. Irwin Alberstat died and Jack Krentzel put in a check for $5000.

First Man: I hear you just had an accident.
Second Man: Yes, it was pretty bad, but I collected $20,000, and my wife who was in the accident with me got $5,000.
First Man: Did she get hurt?
Second Man: No, but I had the presence of mind to kick her in the face during the confusion.

A team of archaeologists were excavating in Israel when they came upon a cave. Written on the wall of the cave were these symbols:

They decided that this was a unique find and the writings were at least three thousand years old. They chopped out the piece of stone and had it brought to the museum where archaeologists from all over the world came to study the symbols.

They held a huge meeting after months of conferences to discuss what they had decided was the meaning of the markings. The President of their society stood up and pointed at the first drawing and said, "This looks like a tomato. We can judge that this was a highly intelligent race as they knew how to grow things to eat. To prove this statement you can see the next drawing resembles a donkey, so, they were even smart enough to have animals help them till the soil. The next drawing looks like a shovel of some sort, which means they even had tools to help them. Even further proof of their high intelligence is the fish which means that had a famine hit the earth whereby the food didn't grow, they would take to the sea for food. The last symbol appears to be the Star of David which means they were evidently Hebrews."

The audience applauded enthusiastically and the President smiled and said, "I'm glad to see that you are all in full agreement with our interpretations."

Suddenly a little old Jewish man stood up in the back of the room and said, "I object to every word. The explanation of what the writings say is quite simple. First of all, everyone knows that Jews don't read from left to right, but from right to left. Now, look again. It says, 'HOLY MACKEREL, DIG THE ASS ON THAT TOMATO.'"

"Yes, my Zeldalah finally got married. I hated to lose her; such a lovely, charming girl. And I am not at all happy with that big mouth she married."

"Why?"

"Well, he's such a boisterous individual, so loud in everything he does. Even at the ceremony, when the rabbi asked him, 'Do you take this woman to be your lawful wedded wife?' he shouted, 'Yeah, yeah, I'll take this broad.' He yelled so loud that my poor sweet daughter almost had a miscarriage!"

She's a cross between the Queen of Sheba and Camille. Sort of a Shlemille.

Delicatessen owner: Did you enjoy the food?
Silverman: I could get more nourishment
biting my lip.

A fellow walked into a Chinese restaurant
and queried the owner:
"What's the specialty in here today?"
"Today we have pizza pie."
"What! In a Chinese restaurant, you have
Italian pizza pie?"
"Sure, this is a Jewish neighborhood!"

Two men were discussing their employers.
"My boss," said the first, "is a no-good
cheap skate. He should only drop dead."
"My boss," smiled the second, "is different.
You can't help liking him, 'cause if you don't
he fires you."

Sigmund Steinberg, the well-known importer from ladies gloves, paid an unexpected call on the rabbi of his temple. That worthy was more than pleased to see his fabulously wealthy congregationer, who more than made up in contributions what he lacked in attendance and religious zeal. This time, however, the trip to temple was for a completely religious, if rather unusual, reason.

"Rabbi," Steinberg commenced after the usual amenities, "I'm here to see you about someone most near and dear to me. Mine own, mine darling, mine three times a champion, Westminster Abie the Third, mine little poodlelah is this coming Tisha Bov 13 years old, and I want, Rabbi, you should Bar Mitzvah him."

The rabbi was completely taken aback. "But my dear Mr. Steinberg, that's impossible. There's never in the history of the Jewish religion been such a thing. It would be a scandal. The temple would be a laughing-stock. My orders would be revoked. The sisterhood would be disbanded. The building campaign would be halted. The gentiles would be hysterical. And the board of directors would have my neck."

Steinberg was unmoved. Without so much as the bat of an eyelash, he addressed the rabbi again. "For the occasion, I am donating to the temple the amount, in cash, of five thousand dollars."

"Mr. Steinberg," the rabbi beamed, "why didn't you tell me in the first place the dog is Jewish?"

Mrs. Goldstein was calling on her neighbor, Mrs. Marks. The ladies were enjoying some tea.

"Mrs. Marks, darling, these cookies you baked are so delicious, I'm afraid I ate already four of them."

Mrs. M. Replying, "Five, but who's counting?"

A young woman was driving along a lonely deserted country road during a thunder and lightening storm when suddenly her car broke down. Looking for help, she came upon a deserted farm house and decided to spend the night there. Just as she fell asleep she heard a noise which woke her. Standing over the bed was a vampire. She grabbed a crucifix from the wall and shoved it in his face, shouting, "The sign of the cross—you are powerless!"

The vampire looked at her and smiled, "It vouldn't help."

Old man Feinstein's relatives gathered for the reading of his will after his death.

"Being of sound mind," read his lawyer, "I spent every last cent before I died."

Frances had just had the house painted. When Harry came home from work, not realizing the paint was still wet, he touched the bedroom wall and left a hand print. The next day, Frances called the painter back to the house. She said, "Mr. Shapiro, I'd like you to see where my husband put his hand last night."

Mr. Shapiro looked at her and sighed, "Mrs. Cohen, to tell you the truth I'm so tired from painting, I don't have the strength for anything else."

The college freshman sent his father a telegram: Rush $25 immediately. Must get a guinea pig.

His father wired back: Sending $50. Get yourself a nice Jewish girl.

Henry went on his first hunting trip. When he got back to his office his partner Morris couldn't wait to hear all about his trip. Henry told him, "Well, I went into the woods with the guide. You know me, two minutes in the woods, I get lost. I'm walking extra quiet, when all of a sudden the biggest bear you ever did see is standing right in front of me. I turn around and run just as fast as I can and that bear, he is running even faster. Just when I feel his hot breath on my neck, he slipped and fell. I jumped over a brook and kept running, but I was losing my breath and sure enough there was that bear getting close to me again. He was almost on top of me, when he slipped again and fell. I kept on running and finally I found myself in the clearing of the woods. The bear was running as fast as he could and I knew I didn't stand a chance. I saw the other hunters and shouted for help and just then the bear slipped and fell again. My guide was able to take aim and he shot the bear and killed him."

Morris said, "Henry, that was quite a story. You are a very brave man. If that would have happened to me, I would have made in my pants."

Henry looked at him and shrugged, "Morris, what do you think the bear was slipping on?"

It all started in front of the Waldorf-Astoria. A mink-befurred, lorgnette-dangling dowager, with trunks and suitcases stacked, was helped into a cab while a second taxi took care of her excess. 'Mrs. Whittlestick," the uniformed doorman said, "wishes to be driven to Pier 8. She's sailing on the S.S. **United States**." The hackie nodded, dropped the flag and beckoned with his little finger to have the baggage car follow. In no longer than it takes to read a union contract, the cab arrived at the pier, the baggage was checked into staterooms A through X, and the lady spoke to the cabby. "If you're single and want to double your income, I'd like to offer you a proposition. See the world through your own windshield. I simply hate hailing strange cabs in strange places. How would you like to drive me around Europe, all expenses paid?"

The hackie's mouth opened, but no words came out. Finally, he nodded. In a few minutes arrangements were made to have the cab hoisted into the hold of the ship, where it remained until the ship berthed in Le Havre. From there they drove to Paris, then Nice, then Monte Carlo, then back to Paris for the channel crossing to England, then to Rome, Berlin and through the Scandinavian countries. Like the cab's two occupants, the meter never stopped running. Eventually, the party retraced its tire treads, the **United States** docked again at the point of origination, Pier 8. The cab was hoisted out of the hold and plunked on land again.

"Well, my good man," the fatigued dowager sighed, paying the $12,457 clicked on the clock, "we're on native soil again, thank goodness. Now will you please drive me home?" "Where is home, ma'am?" the hackie smiled. "It's near Prospect Park, in Brooklyn," his benefactor replied. "Brooklyn!" the hackie snorted, slamming the door. "Are you nuts? Take another cab! Every time I go to Brooklyn I have to come back to Manhattan empty!"

Then there was a zayda of 92 who married a woman of 84. They spent the whole honeymoon getting out of the car.

Solomon had just checked out of a hotel and discovered that his umbrella was missing. By the time he got back to the room, it was already occupied by a newly married couple. Listening at the door, he heard the following conversation:

Groom: Whose lovely eyes are those, darling?

Bride: Yours, sweetheart.

Groom: Whose lovely, gorgeous lips are those?

Bride: Yours, love.

Groom: And whose precious swanlike neck is that, baby?

Bride: Yours, dearest.

At this point Solomon yelled through the keyhole, "When you get to the green striped umbrella—it's mine!"

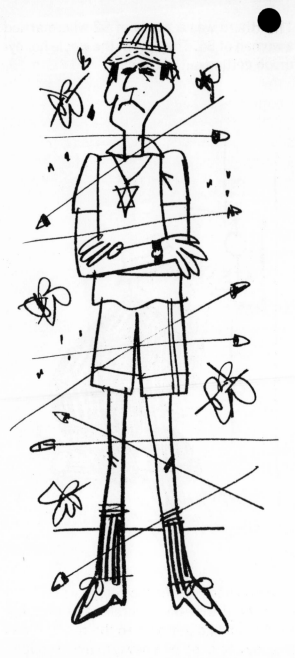

During the period of sniping on the Jaffa sea-front, a Tel Aviv resident saw a dejected-looking friend standing by a wall. "What's wrong, Chaim?" he asked.

"Everything," replied the other. "My wife's left me; my son's been arrested for stealing; my daughter's eloped; my bookkeeper's absconded; and I'm going bankrupt. I'm going to throw myself into the sea."

"Then what are you waiting for?" the first one asked. "It's only fifty yards away."

"How can I cross the square when the Arabs are sniping? I might get killed!"

The detective was probing the mysterious death of a cloak and suit manufacturer. He quizzed his lovely young model. "Can you offer any explanation for your employer's death?" he asked the girl.

"Well, after working for Mr. Finsrel one month," she began, "he gave me a hundred dollar bonus; at the end of the second month a mink coat, and the end of the third month a Cadillac convertible. Then he asked me if I'd make love to him, and how much would I charge him.

"I told him I'd be only too glad, and because he'd been so nice to me, I would only charge him ten dollars—even though I was getting 15 from his salesmen in the office. And that's when he jumped out the window!"

BRITISH GUIDE: (showing place of interest): It was in this room that Lord Wellington received his first commission.
IRVING TOURIST: How much was it?

Thinking he was crossing a field, Solomon Cohen meandered across the country club golf grounds just as a member was teeing off in the distance. The drive sent the ball right to Marcus's eye. Looking around to see who had done it, he spied the golfer coming towards him.

"You can't get away with that," yelled Solomon. "I'm going to sue you in court—I'm going to sue you for five hundred dollars!"
"I said 'fore,'" shouted the golfer.
"I'll take it!" answered Solomon.

Two beautifully groomed women entered a restaurant and passed a table where two men were seated.
First man: Those girls look exactly alike. Are they twins?
Second man: Oh, no. They just use the same plastic surgeon.

One day Irving bought a fine piece of English wool and decided to take it to a custom tailor and have a suit made. He brought it to Lerner & Son and showed it to the designer. He looked at the cloth and said, "Sorry, Irving, you don't have enough cloth here to make a suit."

Disappointed, Irving went across the street to a little old Italian tailor and showed him the cloth. The tailor took his measurements and told him to come back in a week.

A week later, he returned and there was his suit, all finished. He remarked to the little old tailor that he was truly grateful as Lerner had told him that there wasn't even enough cloth there to make a suit. To which the tailor replied, "Enough cloth? Look at my eight-year-old son over there. I even had enough cloth left over to make him a suit!" Enraged, Irving went back across the street to Lerner and said, "Hey, I can't understand it. You told me I didn't have enough goods here to make a suit for myself and the guy across the street not only had enough for a suit for me, but even had enough cloth left over to make his eight-year-old son a suit." The tailor looked at him and shrugged, "Irving, my son is 22."

1st Man: I'll have to buy a new Cadillac this week.
2nd Man: What's wrong with the one you have?
1st Man: The ashtrays are full.

The Jews are certainly an optimistic people ...they cut some of it off even before they know how long it's going to be.

Abe's wife had just died and he was standing over the grave and sobbing uncontrollably. His best friend put his arm around him and said, "Abe, time is a wonderful thing. Believe it or not, some day you'll want to start a new life again and be with people. Maybe even get married again. Listen to me, time heals all wounds."

Abe looked at him and replied, "I know. I know. But tell me Jake, what am I going to do tonight?"

An act walked into the office of an agent who booked the jobs in the classier country clubs of Westchester.

The guy took out his suitcase, opened it, and fifty mice in tuxedos jumped out and set up instruments on top of the case.

The guy snapped his fingers and the little mice played music like the New York Philharmonic. He snapped again, and the mice played better jazz than Stan Getz. Then the mice all went back in the trunk.

The guy said to the agent, "Well?"

The agent said, "I'll see."

"Whatta ya mean," the mice manager exclaimed, "what's the matter with this act?"

The agent said, "Well, they play all right, but the trumpet player looks too Jewish."

Sara: She has teeth just like pearls.
Clara: Yeah . . . she and Pearl got them at the same dentist.

A box manufacturer, who had just returned from an Atlantic City convention, arrived home with a bundle of presents under his arms. When he knocked at his door, his new maid, who had been hired during his absence, answered.

"Would you give these boxes to the lady of the house," he instructed, "and tell her I'm here!"

"You better be quick about it," the maid advised, "she expects her old man home any minute!"

Rich Sam Gold, the hardware magnate, lived on Riverside Drive, and when a friend walked into the house, he was very impressed by the layout and furnishings. But stepping into the living room, he was shocked to see Sam's little three-year-old son holding a hammer in his hand and knocking nails into the piano, the chair, tables, and even the floor.

"That seems like an expensive way for your son to play," he told his host.

"Oh, not at all," Sam assured him. "You see, I don't pay for the nails!"

Two prosperous garment center manufacturers hired a new model. She was a beautiful girl, but she wasn't too bright. The two partners were attracted to the girl, but the interest was not of the paternal nature.

"Look," one told his partner, "being that she's so young and pretty, she might be taken advantage of by some fast talking fellow. I think we ought to take it upon ourselves to teach her what's right and what's wrong."

"O.K.," agreed his partner, "you teach her what's right."

A recently arrived foreigner set himself up in business and found himself one day trying to make a sale to an old America-first type. "Sorry," said the crusty old reactionary, "but I only buy from 100% native born." Somehow the alien was able to convince the old gent that he too descended from a long line of Mayflower ancestors, and closed the sale. As he started to leave, he noticed two large portraits on the wall—one of Washington, the other of Lincoln.

"Fine-looking men," commented the super-salesman, "are they your partners?"

Irving's life was over. His wife had left him and taken the children. He had lost his job. The bank had just foreclosed the mortgage on his house. He decided the only thing left for him to do was to jump off a bridge and kill himself.

He walked to the Brooklyn Bridge and climbed as high as he could and was just about to jump when he heard a voice down below screeching, "Don't jump! I can help you!"

He yelled back, "Who are you?", to which the voice replied, "I am a witch."

Curious, he climbed down and there before him was an ugly old crone. She looked at him and said, "I am a witch and if you do as I say I will grant you three wishes."

He thought to himself, "Things can't be any worse, so what do I have to lose?" So he said, "All right, what do I have to do?"

She said, "Come home with me and spend the night." He went with her to her hovel, and she commanded him to make wild love to her. With great effort he accomplished all her bidding and finally fell asleep in a completely exhausted state. When he woke up, there was the ugly old woman standing in front of him.

He said, "Now that I have done your bidding, old witch, you must keep your part of the bargain and grant me my three wishes."

The hag looked at him and asked, "How old are you?"

He replied, "Forty-two."

The old woman sighed, "Do you mean to tell me that you still believe in witches?"

Sarah wanted a mink coat. Louie refused to buy it for her, claiming a very bad year in business. She told him that she would go out and work for it.

He demanded, "How could you earn money?"

She replied, "The oldest trade in the world," and stormed out of the house. That night, she walked in, all battered and bruised, her clothing in complete disarray, her stockings torn, looking completely bedraggled. She shouted, "You see I can earn money. Look, $24.10."

He looked at her sadly and asked, "Sarah, who gave you the dime?"

She answered, "Everybody."

Father O'Malley and Rabbi Cohen were playing golf. On the third hole, Father O'Malley
hit one into the rough, and he hollered, "Oh,
S---!" And he looked up to heaven and said,
"Dear Lord, I'm terribly sorry. It was an over-
sight." On the fifth hole, he made another
terrible shot into the rough. Again he shouted, "Oh, S---!" Again he looked up to heaven
and said, "Dear Lord, again please excuse
me. I'm terribly sorry." On the ninth hole,
same thing again, into the rough. He holler-
ered "Oh, S---!"

Just then there was a bolt of lightning, and
Rabbi Cohen was struck and killed. A loud
rumbling was heard in heaven and a voice
saying, "Oh, S---!"

Two stuffy old ladies were sitting in a cab.
One turned to the other and said, "These
cab drivers make so much money they all
have homes on the Island." The two women
went on talking about how wealthy the driver
could be. He remained silent. Finally one of
the matrons said to the other—"Humph,
some service. There's not even an ashtray
back here."

At this point the driver turned and said,
"Oh, just throw it on the floor. I have a
woman who comes in once a week."

The Japanese father was admonishing his
daughter about her dating an American
G.I. "Not only is he American, this soldier
of yours, he's JEWISH!" yelled the irate
pater.

"Jewish?" replied his daughter. "What
schmuck told you that?"

SEE A PIN

See a pin and pick it up,
All the day you'll have good luck.
See a pin and let it lay,
Tsuriss!

The heavily jeweled Miami Beach dowager was consulting a leading plastic surgeon.
"What will the operation of lifting my face cost, doctor?" she asked.
"Five thousand dollars, madam."
"That's too much," she protested. "Isn't there something less expensive?"
"You might try wearing a veil," he answered.

The marriage broker took a prospective groom to take a look at a prospective bride. After a look at her, he whispered to the broker: "Why is her ear on her neck—why is one eye on top of the other, and why has she got only one nostril?"
"Obviously you don't care for Picasso!" responded the broker.

Ben Cohen decided to go skiing in Switzerland. No sooner did he reach the top of the ski slope when an avalanche started. He was pushed into a ravine and he sat there hoping that someone would find him. The hotel, knowing he was on the mountain at the time of the avalanche, called the Red Cross and they sent out a rescue party to look for him. After wandering around looking for him for several hours and finding no trace, they started shouting, "Ben Cohen, this is the Red Cross." From the ravine he shouted back, "I already gave through the office."

The old man went to the doctor and said, "Doctor, I feel kind of tired."
The doctor said, "Well, what's bringing it on?"
He replied, "I don't know. I make love to my wife four times a week, and I make love to my girlfriend four times a week. And I make love to my bookeeper four times a week."
The astonished doctor replied, "You make love to your girlfriend four times, your bookkeeper four times, your wife four times! My goodness, man, you better take yourself in hand."
The old man looked at him and said, "I do that four times a week too."

An elderly Jew was run down by a car and lay on the sidewalk, dying. A policeman quickly came on the scene and a priest was called from a nearby church, the cop figuring the old man should get some religious comfort.
Leaning over the victim, the priest intoned. "Do you believe in the Father, the Son and the Holy Ghost?"
The Jew rolled his eyes and groaned, "I'm laying here dying and he's asking me riddles!"

The local synagogue was holding a raffle to raise money for a new building. The third prize winner was announced and he won a beautiful color television set. Then they announced the second prize winner. It was Mr. Epstein. Up he walked to collect his prize and you can imagine his surprise when he found out it was a sponge cake.

"A sponge cake! Who wants a sponge cake? I spent $100 on a raffle ticket, third prize is a color TV and I win a sponge cake? I ain't gonna take a sponge cake!"

"Shh," said the man next to him. "The sponge cake was baked by the rabbi's wife."

"Screw the rabbi's wife," said Mr. Epstein.

"Sssshhh," said the man, "that's the first prize!"

Max was sitting in his office when the intercom buzzed. Max flipped the switch and his partner Sam in the next room said, "Listen, I got an important telegram."

Max: So go ahead, read.

Sam: Wait, the secretary's here, she'll read it.

Max: Go ahead, darling.

Secretary: Must have ten gross...stop... Ladies' gloves...stop...Assorted colors... stop..Pay top price...stop...

Max: Sam, will you leave that girl alone and let her read the telegram...this is business!

Sammy's cousin Hymie from Cincinnati was visiting him in the Bronx. Hymie asked, "What's the population here, Sam? Is everybody Jewish?"

Sammy said, "Well, we got about 15,000 Jews, and maybe 2,000 Irish and Italian cops, firemen, and garbage collectors. How's by you in Cincinnati?"

"Funny thing," said Hymie, "we got about 15,000 Jews, too, but about 150,000 gentiles."

"Oy," cried Sammy, "that's some rich community! You really **need** so many in help?"

How can you tell the difference between a Jew and an Italian? The Jew is the one in the Italian suit.

Kindly Dr. Goldstein was noted for his earthy, everyday approach to the practice of medicine.

"Could you tell me, Doctor," asked a new and nervous father-to-be of the sagely medic, "how soon after the baby is born can my wife and I have intercourse?"

Peering over his pince-nez, the aging physician replied, "That depends, my boy, on whether she's in a ward or a private room."

Old man Finkelstein had to have open heart surgery. He called the medical society and asked for the best doctor in New York for this operation. They recommended the country's most famous surgeon and old man Finkelstein went right to his office and arranged to have the operation. The operation was a complete success and Finkelstein made a quick recovery. After he was home from the hospital, he received a bill from the doctor for $1500. He called the doctor and asked to see him.

Finkelstein looked at the doctor and said, "Doctor, I'm an old man. For me to give you $1500 would mean spending almost all of my life's savings."

The doctor said, "Alright, Mr. Finkelstein. I normally get $1500 for this operation, but under the circumstances, I'll take $750."

Finkelstein, looking very sad, replied, "Doctor, $750 is still a lot of money to an old man like me. After all, I don't work anymore and it would take me a long time to save that much money again."

The doctor, completely frustrated, answered, "Okay. How about $200?"

Finkelstein answered, "$200 I know doesn't sound like much to you, but to me it's like a million dollars."

The doctor, completely annoyed, looked at Finkelstein and said, "You win. I won't charge you a thing for this operation—it's on the house. There's only one thing I would like to know. Before you came to me, you knew I was one of the most expensive surgeons in the United States, so, why did you?"

Finkelstein replied, "When it comes to my health, money's no object."

The tired dress manufacturer had been working extremely hard. Sitting at his desk, he chewed on his pen and said, "The heck with it. Tonight I'm gonna get a young chick, enjoy a little bit."

He grabbed hold of his nineteen-year-old secretary, wined her and dined her. As tired as he was, he tried to keep up a steady conversation, and be pleasant. Around twelve o'clock, he said, "Let's go to my apartment." They arrived. "Take off the clothes," he said. They got in bed. He looked at her and said, "Spread the legs."

"Okay," she replied. "Not yours," he said, "mine!"

Artie was advised by his doctor that he had a very rare disease and the only remedy was a daily glass of fresh mother's milk. They found a young lady that was willing to sell her milk and Artie sat down and nursed on her breast. After about five minutes, the woman looked at him and breathlessly asked, "Is there anything else you would like?"

Artie replied, "If it wouldn't be too much trouble, maybe a cookie."

Two accountants were having lunch together. One of the men asked the other why
he was so preoccupied. "It's my crazy wife.
She told me that last night she dreamt she
was married to a multi-millionaire," was the
reply.
"Brother, you're lucky," sighed his friend.
"My wife dreams that in the daytime!"

Jake had made a success and finally was
able to join a nice country club that had just
recently started to admit members who
were not at least third generation Ameri-
cans. He was invited to join a golf foursome
and as they played, the other three men
were reminiscing about the crash of 1929
and the effect it had on their childhoods.
Jake joined in the conversation and told
them that his father was completely wiped
out in the crash. They were surprised to
hear this and one asked how it happened,
to which Jake replied that his father was on
Wall Street when somebody jumped out of
a window and completely demolished his
pushcart.

What's the plural for Yenta? Hadassah.

A young delinquent walked into a grocery store and held it up. As he was going out, the grocer pulled out a gun and shot him in the arm. The kid ran four blocks, slipped in a puddle, ripped his pants on a nail, and finally, with a last breath, staggered to his home and rang the bell. His mother opened the door, saw her bedraggled son and said, "First you'll eat—then we'll talk."

Izzy was put up for membership in a very ultra, snobbish club. Before the admissions committee, he answered all the questions satisfactorily. For the last question they asked him, 'Did your parents come from Russia?''

''No, they didn't,'' came his prompt reply. He was admitted to membership, but in two weeks he was back before them on charges.

''You acted on false pretenses. You lied to us. We asked you if your parents came from Russia and you said they didn't!''

''Well, they didn't—they're still there!''

The battle in the Crimea was at its height when a Czarist officer addressed his troops. ''The time has come! We are going to charge the enemy. It will be man against man in hand-to-hand combat!''

In the regiment was a Jew who hated the war and the Czar equally. ''Please, Captain, show me my man!'' he cried. ''Maybe I can come to an understanding with him!''

Sadie Glick went to the cemetery to visit her husband Sol. After wandering around the graveyard for about an hour she still was unable to find her dearly beloved Sol's grave. In complete frustration, she went to the office and asked if they would direct her to Sol's plot. They searched their records and they were unable to find a record of a Sol Glick being buried in the cemetery.

When informed of this, Sadie demanded to look through their records. She thumbed through every Glick and finally rested her finger on a listing which said, "Sadie Glick" and shouted with great glee, "That's it!"

The custodian looked at her and said, "Sorry madam, that can't be it, you said that you were looking for your husband Sol, right?"

She answered, "That's my Sol for you. He always put everything in my name."

When a Jewish boy gets bar-mitzvahed in China, he says, "Today, I am a man-darin."

It was the night of their 50th wedding anniversary. After returning home from the big party given in their honor, Bertha turned to Sam and asked, "Sam, remember how we made love the night we got married? How about trying again for old times sake?"
Sam answered, "Of course, my darling."
Sam kept trying and trying, and before Bertha realized what happened, she fell asleep. When she woke up it was morning. Sam opened his eyes and looked at her and Bertha asked, "Tell me, I fell asleep. How did you make out?"

What word beginning in "A" means prince in Jewish? A doctor.

Algonquin Cohen, very big in ladies' and kiddies' millinery, was showing off his fabulous estate to a visiting buyer. The lady, very obviously impressed, exclaimed, "What an enormous swimming pool!"
This, my dear," expounded Algonquin, "is always filled with warm water for my guests who only like to swim in warm water!"
As they walked on, the visitor gasped at the sight of another Olympic-sized pool. Al chuckled, "Filled always with cold water, for my friends who only like to swim in cold water. But wait, you haven't seen anything!"
Sure enough, at the next turn of the flagstone walk, was a third pool. "But Mr. Cohen," said the buyer, on closer examination, "this pool is empty!"
"Certainly," said Cohen proudly, "that's for my friends who don't like to swim!"

Three old ladies were sitting on a porch in the Catskills having a glass of shnapps. The first lady said, "Such a rich son I got. His house in Riverdale has 52 gorgeous rooms and not one, but two swimming pools built into the house."

The second lady said, "My son, with brains he's loaded. He's a dentist, a doctor and a brain surgeon, and now just for fun he's graduating law school."

The third lady said, "So my son, what a built he's got on him. That boy has such a penis, twelve birds can stand in a row on it without even touching each other."

But around the third glass of schnapps, the first lady said, "Look, I gotta be honest, my son's fancy house, maybe it just has nine or ten rooms and maybe there's just a wading pool for the kiddies in the backyard."

The second lady said, "So OK, so if you really want to know, my son couldn't get into medical school or law school; he just happens to have a couple of lawsuits on his hands."

The third lady said, "Girls, as long as everybody's being honest, I'm going to tell you the truth, too. The bird on the end of my son's penis, he has to stand on one leg!"

Once a traveling salesman died suddenly in a small southern village. The local coroner made the usual examination, found the man's business card in his pocket, and sent this telegram:

"It appears that the man who died in our town was named Irving Goldfarb and that he was employed by your firm. We are holding his body. What is the first thing you want us to do?"

The answering telegram came immediately: "Please search his pockets for orders. Will report more fully later."

A pseudo-intellectual visited an eminent Talmudic scholar and dinned into his ears his uninspired interpretations on the teachings of the Prophets. His patience at the breaking point, the scholar muttered under his breath, "Too bad, too bad, you didn't live in the time of Maimonides!"

The dullard glowed at the comment. "Thank you, thank you, Rabbi," he beamed. "Tell me—why do you think I should have known Maimonides?"

"Because," snapped the Rabbi, "had you known Maimonides, you could have bored him—not me!"

Joe Levy went to a leading mountain resort for a week's vacation. That night, when he ordered dinner the waiter told him that he highly recommended the chicken soup. Joe replied, "I hate soup. I never eat soup. I couldn't care less." He ate his dinner, played cards, and retired to his room early and fell asleep.

In the middle of the night, the man in the room below his took sick suddenly and the house doctor recommended that they get a nurse and give him an enema. The nurse arrived, and in error, entered Joe Levy's room and before he even realized what was happening to him, gave him the enema and left. When he got back to New York, his friends asked him how he had liked the hotel. He said, "It was very nice, but if you ever go there and the waiter suggests that you eat the soup, eat it, otherwise they shove it into you anyway."

Tomashefsky, the great Yiddish actor, was full of both the vanity and sexual vigor usually attributed to that breed. One afternoon, he deigned to give the majesty of his person and his bed to a very poor and wistful young thing. Rather pleased with the girl's performance, the great one handed her a couple of tickets for his theater.

"Thank you very much, sir," she said pleadingly, "but I need bread, bread!"

"You want bread," roared Tomashefsky, "next time, screw a baker!"

Judge—"You say the unwritten law would have justified you in killing Mr. Cohen, and you had pulled a gun on him. Yet you did not fire. Why?"

Mr. Goldstein—"Well, Judge, when I pointed my pistol at him, he says, 'How much you want for that gun?' I ask you, Judge, could I kill a man when he was talking business?"

One night in a resort hotel there was a loud argument in one of the rooms that could be heard all over the place.

"What's all the noise about?" asked a guest.

"They're having a battle of wits," said the desk clerk.

"A battle of wits?' asked the guest. "Who's in the room?"

"Markowitz, Lefkowitz and Horowitz," said the desk clerk.

People in Israel tell jokes about their economic situation. One tells about an Israeli who died and went to Hell. He found things so idyllic there, he was disappointed when he found himself suddenly "banished" to Heaven. So he prevailed on St. Peter to send him back below. On his return he was starved and put to work.

"What's the matter?" he asked. "When I was here before you fed me well and let me rest."

"Well," an answer came back, "three weeks ago you were a tourist. Now you're an immigrant."

You may not believe this, but there's a little Southern town where the entire population consists of two Jewish families and a dog . . . and the dog is the mayor!

Mr. Cohen belonged to an organization with many social benefits. Each person in the club was asked to buy a plot at a reduced rate—sort of a group plan so they could have have a place to live when they died. When the organization found that it wasn't paying off too well, they asked the president to talk to the delinquent members.

Cohen was first to be called. "You bought a plot twenty-five years ago," the president began, "and you haven't paid for it yet." The member looked askance. "I didn't use it," he answered.

"So who stopped you?" was the snappy reply.

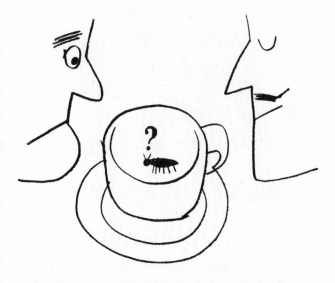

"What does this mean?" cried a customer at the downtown delicatessen. "There's a roach in the bottom of my teacup."

"Don't ask me, lady," snapped the waiter. "If you want your fortune told, go to a gypsy tearoom."

The wealthiest member of a very wealthy temple was famous, or rather infamous, for his yearly contribution of a mere five thousand dollars. Year in, year out, regardless of the magnanimity of less affluent members, he announced his usual five thousand. This year, though, was the year the temple decided it needed another swimming pool, replete with sauna baths, cabanas, and all the other necessities of Jewish community life. Accordingly, the fund-raising committee was putting on the hardest drive in the history of the temple. Naturally, the aforementioned stingy Steingarten was target number one.

He was bombarded, he was harangued, he

was haunted night and day by the committee members; his telephone, whenever it rang, sang out a call from one of the members; his mail was thickened with their written pleas and admonitions; his ears were threatened with their verbal ones. There wasn't a customer his company did business with who wasn't brought into the fray. Finally, Steingarten relented.

The grapevine soon carried the news that at

the fund-raising dinner-dance, the word would be given of the entirely unprecedented amount, to be announced by Steingarten himself.

The big night finally arrived. The befurred, bejewelled, regally attired congregation stirred impatiently throughout the meal, the entertainment, the opening ceremonies. An expectant hush settled over the hall as the pledging started. By unspoken assent, Steingarten's name would be the last to be called, in order to sustain interest and not to embarrass the smaller donors. The effect was pure theater.

"And now," purred the voice of the m.c., "we come to our beloved member Carlyle Steingarten. Mr. Steingarten, your contribution?"

In stentorian tones, his voice never wavering, Steingarten rose from his seat announcing, with right arm outstretched, "I pledge...one million dollars!"

"Ohhh," breathed the crowd, but Steingarten continued, "payable for tax purposes, at the rate of five thousand dollars a year!"

Milton called his doctor because he had a terrible headache and an upset stomach. The telephone answering service answered and Milton explained what was wrong with him. The operator told him to take two aspirins and call back the following day.

Milton woke up the next morning and dialed the doctor's number again. The same operator answered and he told her that he still didn't feel better. She told him to take two more aspirins and call back that evening.

He waited until 6:00, couldn't stand it any longer, and dialed the doctor's number again and Dr. Bleicher himself was on the other end of the phone. He asked Milton if he could be of help, to which Milton replied, "If you don't mind I'd rather talk to your operator now as she knows all about my case."

When advised that the coffin she admired so much (to bury her husband in) would cost $6000, Mrs. Schwartz replied, "For that much money, I'd rather bury him in a Cadillac."

"How would you feel if you had all of Rockefeller's money?"
"I'd be richer than Rockefeller."
"How would you be richer?"
"I'd still keep my candy store."

A patient, bent and with every symptom of suffering, came into the doctor's office. The M.D. found it impossible to diagnose the case, went into his private office to look at the medical books for some form of clue, but could find nothing to go by. He had to give the patient a decision, so he asked him, "Did you ever have this before?"
"Yes."
"Just as I thought—you got it again," replied the doctor.

"This book," said the saleman, "will do half your work."
"Fine," said the dress manufacturer, "I'll take two of them."

She was a sweet young thing; he was a fast-rising account executive with the well-known Madison Avenue advertising agency, Bittner, Berman, Dirstein and Osman. Everyone thought it was an ideal marriage. But alas, there was a problem...with sex. The honeymoon hadn't even begun.
"B-b-being an advertising man," she sobbed to a friend, "all he does every night is sit on the edge of the bed and tell me how wonderful it's going to be!"

The assistant manager, noticing the frown on the store owner's face, said, "You sure look worried!"
"Listen," replied the manager, "I have so many worries that if something happens to-day, I won't have time to worry about it for another two weeks."

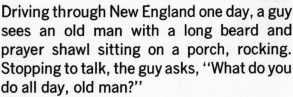

Driving through New England one day, a guy sees an old man with a long beard and prayer shawl sitting on a porch, rocking. Stopping to talk, the guy asks, "What do you do all day, old man?"

"Me, I just sit here and rock—it's my job—and everybody driving by knows it's a kosher house, they don't need to hang out a sign."

Driving through Tennessee one day, the same guy sees the same old man with the beard rocking on a porch. He stops and asks him what he's doing there and gets the same story. And then, months later, the same thing happens in Minnesota. "After all," says the old man, "who would know it's a kosher house in Minnesota if it weren't for me?"

Then, about a year later, the guy takes a big trip to Israel and drives down a street in Tel Aviv. There he sees the same old man rocking on a porch. "For God's sake," the guy says, "You mean to tell me they need to pay you **here** so people should know it's a kosher house?"

"No," says the old man, "here I'm the golf pro!"

Sam's wife was such a meticulous house-keeper, that when he'd get up at night to go to the john, she'd make the bed!

A Hollywood director, whose first experience in America was cloak-and-suiting, was going over a part in his picture with a well-known actor.

"You're new at this college, see?" he explained. "It's your first job teaching. The dean is taking you around the campus, then up the hall to show you the classroom. This you've studied for all your life! You choke up. Your chest swells. Tears come to your eyes as you look on the door and see those wonderful words in big letters: 'JOHN SMITH, PROFESSOR FROM ENGLISH'!"

Two Jewish stock brokers met and one told the other: "Buy U.S. Rubber. It's going to amalgamate with Fanny Farmer. They're going to produce a falsie that melts in your mouth."

The funeral was over. Still sobbing, Goldberg, the new widower, followed his late wife's sister-in-law into the waiting limousine. As the big car passed through the cemetery gates, the sister-in-law was horrified by Goldberg's hand, which was slowly but passionately creeping up her leg.

Her body still racked with sobs of bereavement, she screamed, "Goldberg, you fiend, you monster, you animal! My sister isn't yet cold in her grave! What's the matter with you?"

In a voice shaking with emotion, Goldberg replied, "In my grief, do I know what I'm doing?"

A husband rushed home and announced to his wife: "Darling, we don't have to move to a more expensive apartment—the landlord just raised the rent."

Oscar Moskowitz and Sidney Margolis had a profitable little business going importing artificial flowers for the ladies dress trade. Mainly, it was profitable due to their seldom, if ever, paying Uncle Sam taxes. But to their loft came, as it must to all men, the agents of the Revenue Service. Finding Oscar in charge, as Sidney was on a buying trip, the first agent tried to explain the nature of the visit.

"Mr. Moskowitz, you people are doing business and failing to report to the government."

Oscar turned purple. "Report? What report? What's to report?" he demanded.

"Well," the agent replied, "first of all we'd like to know about your dependencies, that is, your family exemptions."

Oscar proceeded to tell them all about Harriet, his wife, dependant number one, and all the trouble and aggravation she had been giving him lately. Then he got to his son, and described in great detail how Freddie had gotten this girl in trouble and the ensueing problems from that scene. Dependant number three, his daughter Marjorie, a good girl, but no beauty, and how much she was costing him. Not quite family, certainly, the shicksa in the stockroom, but still a drain on Oscar's finances.

Finally, after absorbing as much of the detail of Oscar's private life as he could stand, the agent said, "Mr. Moskowitz, let's forget all that for a moment and concentrate on the business itself."

Replies Oscar, "Like what, exactly?"

Replies the agent, who by this time was beginning to sound a little like Oscar himself, "Like, how much business you're doing, what the assets are worth, how much profit you made..."

"What," screamed Oscar hysterically, "are you crazy? I don't even tell my partner that!"

To hell with expense. Give the parakeet another seed!

A renowned waiter at Lindy's died, and some of his show business regulars were so saddened by his loss that they decided to visit a medium to try and communicate with their long-lost friend.

The medium advised, "Just knock on the table as you did when he was alive and he shall appear."

The friends knocked on the table but the waiter didn't appear. They knocked again and still no waiter. Finally they banged and banged on the table and called his name.

Then, in a puff of smoke, the waiter appeared in his uniform with a cloth over his arm. "Why didn't you first appear when you heard us knocking?" they asked.

"It wasn't my table," answered the waiter.

A conscientious bookkeeper showed up at his office one morning looking completely worn-out.

"You must have had a big evening," said one of his co-workers.

"It isn't that," yawned the bookkeeper. "I couldn't go to sleep, so I started counting sheep. But I made a mistake, and it took me all night to find it."

The distraught young man was perched on the 40th floor ledge of a midtown hotel, and threatening to jump. The closest the police could get was the roof of an adjacent building a few feet below. However, all pleas to the man to return to safety were to no avail. A priest from the nearest parish was summoned, and he hastened to the scene.

"Think, my son," he intoned to the would-be suicide, "think of your mother and father who love you."

"Aw, they don't love me," the man replied, "I'm jumping!"

"No! Stop!" cried the priest. "Think of the woman who loves you!"

"Nobody loves me! I'm jumping!" came the response.

"But think," the priest implored, "think of Jesus and Mary and Joseph who love you!"

"Jesus, Mary and Joseph?" the man queried, "who are they?"

At which point the cleric yelled back, "Jump, you Jew bastard, jump!"

Harry Schultz was a traveling salesman for a large dry goods company. Held over in a little Alabama town one night, he overheard plans for a scheduled meeting of the Ku Klux Klan at midnight.

Promptly at twelve, Harry presented himself at the door of the klavern. A hooded figure stepped out and demanded: "What do you want, Jew-boy?"

Frightened, Harry stammered in his native New Yorkese, "I only wanted to come in for a minute."

The hooded hulk bellowed, "We don't let no Jews join the Klan."

Harry answered, "So who wants to join? I only want to see the linen buyer!"

Every year, some high dignitaries of the Church travel from Rome to Israel and a time-honored ceremony is reenacted. One of the chief rabbis hands a jewel-covered scroll to a visiting priest who holds the scroll for a minute, shakes his head and then returns it to the rabbi until the next year.

This year, however, the rabbi and the priest involved in the ceremony grew curious about the scroll and, between them, decided to open it. They finally got the jeweled covering off, then unrolled yards and yards of yellowed parchment with long columns of numbers on it and some blurred words. Putting on his bifocals, the rabbi finally managed to read the ancient Hebrew letters.

It was the bill for the Last Supper.

A man went to Florida for his health but after two weeks he died and his body was shipped back home for the funeral. Two friends looked at him as he lay in the casket.
1st friend: Doesn't he look wonderful?
2nd friend: Yes, I think those two weeks in Miami did him a world of good.

Two old friends met on the street at Miami Beach. One asked the other where she was staying, to which she replied that year's newest hotel. She, in turn, asked her friend where she was staying to which she answered, "My hotel is so new, we are still under construction."

An indulgent son sent his mother a brilliantly colored talking parrot for a Chanukah gift. He called her a few days later and asked, "Well, Mama, what did you think of the bird?"
"Oh, Sonny," she replied, smacking her lips, "it was delicious!"
"Mama!" he exclaimed, "You weren't supposed to cook it. That bird spoke seven languages!"
"So, nu," she came back, "why didn't he say something?"

It was a terrible night. The rain was coming down in sheets. The wind was blowing fiercely and visibility was almost nil. The millinery salesman was having trouble driving through the Mississippi back roads.

"This is a rough one," he told his pet dog, who accompanied him on all his trips. "Looks like we're in for it!"

But no sooner had he spoken than he spotted a small motel. He couldn't have been happier. He drove up and parked in front of the office, picked up his pup and ran in.

"I'd like a room for tonight," he told the desk clerk.

"Sorry, mister," said the redneck at the desk. "We're all filled up."

"I could sleep on the sofa," suggested the salesman.

"That's where Ah sleep."

"But you can't turn me out on a night like this," protested the salesman.

The cracker simply shrugged, and the salesman realized it was useless to plead. He turned to go, but the cracker stopped him before he got to the door.

"Just a minute, mister," he said. "Leave the pup here. Ah wouldn't turn a dog out on a night like this!"

He was a salesman and she was a purchasing agent for a leading manufacturer. They met whenever he came to sell his latest items, and eventually he proposed. She accepted.

For their honeymoon, they went to Acupulco. They arrived on Friday night and had a wonderful time. Saturday and Sunday, too, were blissful days that he would never forget.

But when he awoke on Monday morning, she was gone. He quickly dressed, ran downstairs and searched all over for her. Not finding a trace of her, he packed his bags and took the next flight back to New York.

First he went home, but she wasn't there. Then he went to his office and sat down, brooding over his fate.

"What's the matter," asked one of his co-workers. "Why are you so blue?"

Heartbroken, Harry told him about the events of the last few hours.

"Don't worry," his friend reassured him, "you know she never sees salesmen on Mondays!"

The wife of a prominent plastics manufacturer suspected that her husband was carrying on with one of his pretty young employees.

Accordingly, she went to a detective agency with her problem. The agency took the job. They put an investigator to work, and within a week he discovered that the wife's suspicions were well-founded. Hubby was very sweet on a cute blonde steno.

"I'll get him," the wife told the head of the agency. "How much would it cost to get concrete evidence—enough to sue?"

The agency chief made a few notes on his pad. "With one investigator, a photographer and a witness, it will come out to $500."

The wife nodded. "Get started right away! I think I can borrow that much from my boyfriend."

She was supposed to be vacationing for her health, but so it shouldn't be a total loss, she was keeping an eye peeled for a young man for Charlotte, her eldest.

One afternoon, seated by the pool, it occurred to her that the handsome young lifeguard might be a prospect.

"Young man," she called, "come talk to an old lady." When he was standing by her chair, she said, "Sit down, you look like a nice young man. I'd like you to meet my daughter."

"What does she look like?" asked the youth.

"She's a wonderful girl," gushed Mrs. Finster, "and very intelligent. She graduated from Long Island University with honors."

'Oh, yes? And is she good-looking?'

"And now she's got a job teaching on Long Island. She makes all her own clothes and she can cook better than her own mother."

"She sounds like a nice girl. But is she pretty?"

"Her uncle in the clothing business gave her $25,000 when she graduated, and..."

"Is she here with you now, Mom?"

Definition of a schmuck: that's a guy who gets out of the shower to take a leak.

"The main thing to remember," swift Sidney Ginsburg, an advertising executive said to a member of his staff, "is that repetition, repetition, repetition is the key! You have a product to sell. Keep harping on it in every possible way, cram it down people's throats —make yourself sickening and repulsive if you have to, but don't forget to repeat and repeat and repeat! It's the only way to get results!"

"Yes, sir," the employee replied in a meek voice.

"And now, what was it you came in to see me about?" the genius of the agency business asked.

"Well, Sid," came the reply, "a raise! A raise! A raise! A raise! A raise! A raise! A raise!"

Stella Schoenfeld arrived in Miami on a day in which the temperature had zoomed well over 100. As she got out of her car, she was overcome by the heat and fainted. A crowd of concerned bystanders gathered around her.

"Get a glass of water!" shouted one.

"Get a doctor!" screamed another.

"Open up her mink!" yelled the third.

There was a long line waiting in the early morning in front of a clothing store that advertised a special sale. A man walked to the front of the line. The people grabbed him and pushed him to the end. Again he walked to the front and they beat him up and shoved him to the back. Once more he headed for the front and this time they kicked him and pushed him into the gutter.

He got up, brushed himself off, and said to a man at the end of the line, "If they do that one more time—I don't open the store."

A priest went into a tailor's shop and ordered a new suit. When he asked how much it cost the tailor said, "There's no charge. I never charge the clergy." So the next day the priest sent the tailor a beautiful crucifix. Then a rabbi went into the tailor's shop and ordered a new suit. When he asked how much it cost the tailor said, "There's no charge. I never charge rabbis." So the next day the rabbi sent the tailor two more rabbis.

A Jewish wife is able to forgive and forget —except she'll never forget what she forgave.

May and Herman had an only daughter, Fanny. One day Fanny came home and announced to her family that she was converting to Catholicism and becoming a nun. Her parents told her that if she did from that day on she was dead to them and even went as far as to sit Shivah for her.

Two years past and the telephone rang early one morning. Herman answered the phone and a woman's voice told him that she was the Mother Superior of the Convent in which his daughter Fanny had been living and Fanny had died.

Herman replied, "I have no daughter. She died two years ago."

The Mother Superior said, "Please sir, I know you feel bitter, but, we must know what you would like us to do with your daughter's body."

Herman asked, "Tell me, what happens when a girl becomes a nun?" The Mother Superior then went into detail on all of the ritual involved and explained how his daughter was married to Jesus Christ.

Herman said, "If, according to you, she is now married to Jesus Christ, call up my son-in-law and ask him where to send the body."

Becky fell into the hands of a gypsy fortune teller. One day, the gypsy promised to hold a seance and bring Becky's grandmother back from the great beyond. Becky was thrilled because her grandmother could advise her what to do with her money.

That night, the seance was held. Becky and the gypsy joined hands and suddenly a spirit appeared before Becky.

Becky said, "Grandma, how are things?"

A voice replied, "Wonderful."

Becky asked, "Are you happy in your new surroundings?"

The voice replied, "I couldn't be happier, my child. Is there something important that you called me back here to ask?"

Becky said, "Yes, but first tell me, Grandma, when did you learn to speak English?"

He called in his best salesman and laid it down to him: "I know business is bad all over, but I want you should go on the road and get some orders."

The salesman gave him an argument: "What, go on the road at a time like this to get orders? Why, I'd have to cry with actual tears to soften their hearts!"

The boss was adamant: "That's exactly what I want you should do—with actual tears, I want you to cry!" He couldn't budge the boss, so he went on the road.

After a month, he came back without a single order.

The boss yelled: "What?—not ONE order? Did you cry with tears, like I told you to do?"

"I'll say I cried. Such tears you never saw come out of a person."

"And you got no orders?"

"No, but I got forty dollars for myself."

At Bergdorf Goodman one afternoon, an employee approached one of the department heads and whispered: "I just glanced in the fitting room. There's a customer in there trying on a blouse and she has a blindfold on!"

"Naturally," said the customer-oriented executive. "She's getting it for her husband to give to her for her birthday and it's supposed to be a surprise."

A group of dress salesmen were in a bar and the discussion turned to who was the greatest inventor. One said Fulton, who invented the steamboat; another said Edison; another, Marconi; and still another said the Wright brothers.

Finally, one of them turned to a quiet man who had not given his opinion. "What do you think?" he was asked.

"Well," he said, "the man who invented 6% interest was nobody's fool."

Husband: A neighbor just told me that the milkman who delivers here makes love to every woman in this building but one.

Wife: Yeah, it's that stuck-up Mrs. Lerner on the third floor.

"What in the world happened to you?" a fellow asked a friend who was walking on crutches.

"Got hit by a bus a couple of months ago," the man said.

"Two months ago?" his friend asked. "And you still aren't able to walk without crutches?"

"Well," said the man, "it's this way. Markowitz, my doctor says I can walk without them, but, Moskowitz, my lawyer, thinks I had better keep using them for a while."

A friend got married and Phil was worried as to what to buy him for a wedding present. Somebody suggested that he give the groom cash. "No, no," he replied, "I can't get it wholesale."

Harry Rothstein was telling how he attained his fortune. "I never hesitate," he said, "to give my wife full credit for her assistance." "And just how much did she help?" he was asked.

"Frankly," confessed the wealthy one, "I was curious to see if there was any income she couldn't live beyond."

A tailor who suffered from insomnia agreed to try the old remedy of counting sheep. Next morning he turned up for business more tired than ever. "What a night," he confessed. "I counted three thousand sheep. Then I figured that was eight thousand yards of wool. That would make 2500 suits—and where would I get all that lining?"

Did you hear about the delicatessen owner hiring midget waiters so his sandwiches would look bigger?

Sam Klein had worked for Funk and Wagnall's for 35 years and had never had a raise. He went to the head of personnel and demanded to see Mr. Funk. He was ushered into Mr. Funk's office, and he looked at his boss and said, "Mr. Funk, I have worked for you for 35 years. I have never been late. I have never missed a day at work. I have been a faithful loyal employee. In all the years I have been here I have never had a raise in salary and I think that it is time that I got one now."

Mr. Funk looked at him and said, "I have news for you. You never got a raise and you're still not going to get a raise."

Klein looked at his boss and shouted, "Mr. Funk, you're a prink."

"Well, my boy," asked Howie's father, "how do you like being married?" His newly-wed son blushed scornfully. "Married? Ha, some marriage. I married a nun."

"What do you mean, a nun?" his father queried.

"None in the morning, none at night," replied the groom.

"Well," sighed papa, "you'll come for dinner Friday night, you'll meet the Mother Superior."

A Christian, a Mohammedan and a Jew were asked, "What would you do if a tidal wave drove the ocean waters over your land?"

"We would die with the sign of the cross and beg the Lord to open for us the pearly gates of Heaven," said the Christian.

"We would pray to Allah and be consoled in our Kismet. As it is destined to be, so is it," said the Moslem.

"We," said the Jew, "would learn to live under water."

Francine had worked all year in a sweat shop and saved her money diligently to go to the resort of the year. The first night at the hotel, she met Sol and he romanced her the whole week that she was there and after seducing her, promised to call on her in the city. Poor Fran waited for his call, which never came. Heartsick and disillusioned, after not hearing from him, she summoned all her courage and decided to call him. She remembered that he had told her that he was an executive with the Swift & Armour Meat Packing Company.

She called Swift & Armour and asked to talk to their Vice-President Sol Geck. The switchboard operator told her that there was nobody in their executive offices by that name, but, connected her with personnel who she said might be able to tell her if there was a Sol Geck working for Swift & Armour.

Personnel looked through all of their records and finally located a Sol Geck, who worked in their Yonkers factory as a Pheasant Plucker. Fran exclaimed upon hearing this, "That's him. He was pleasant and a good dancer too."

They had been quarrelling for the twenty-five years of their married life. On their silver anniversary, she said, "Well, how are we gonna celebrate?"

"How about two minutes of silence?" he suggested.

An elderly lady was introduced to a Dr. Klein at a party. At her first opportunity she cornered the gentleman and said, "Doctor, I'm so glad to meet you. Let me ask you a question. Lately I get a terrible pain here in my side when I raise my arm like this. What should I do about it?"

The gentleman answered, "I'm very sorry, madam, but you see, I'm not that kind of a doctor. I happen to be a doctor of economics."

"Oh," said the old lady. "So tell me, should I sell my General Motors?"

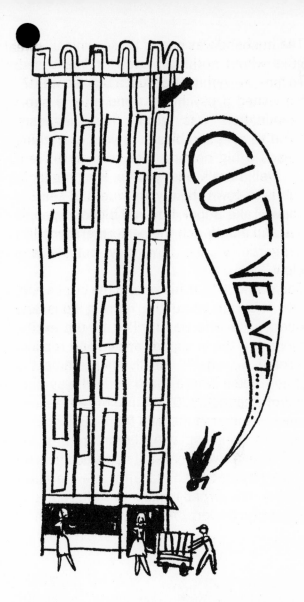

Solomon and Irving were both partners in the dress business. They had the worst season of their careers and were at a complete loss as to what to make that would sell. There wasn't a dress to be cut in their cutting room. They both decided the only way out to leave their families any money was to agree to a suicide pact. They drew straws and Solomon was to jump first. Solomon jumped out the 30th floor window and as he was falling he noticed every cutting room on every floor he passed was busy. He yelled back to Irving, "Don't jump! Cut velvet!"

The husband was one of those cynical, sour guys whom nothing moved or impressed. To him, everything was just a big "so what?" He visited a psychiatrist and after a short examination was given this diagnosis: "You're cold and blasé. To you, everything means a big nothing. You're married, eh? . . . well, here's what you do. Ringling's circus is in town, take your wife and see the show. Take a look how red-blooded people live and act. Watch the performers who live dangerously; see how they pulsate and glow."

The schnook took his wife to the circus. Out into the ring came the roaring lions and tigers. The wife was thrilled by the excitement, but the husband yawned and replied, "Yeah? So what?" Finally there came the grand finale where the daredevil was shot out of a cannon 300 feet into the air, turned several somersaults, and then, pulling out a clarinet, began playing before hitting the net. The crowed roared its appreciation for the act but the husband, after a few minutes of thought, turned to his wife and grunted in a bored manner, "A Benny Goodman, he's not!"

The owner of a wholesale wool business insisted on having all his checks dated ahead. When he died, his tombstone read; "HERE LIES SIDNEY HELLER. DIED JUNE 5TH AS OF JULY 2ND."

Morris was dying of smallpox. He turned to his devoted wife and said, "Sadie, I am dying. Get me a priest."

Sadie said, "Morris, you have been an orthodox Jew all of your life, why at a time like this should you get it into your head to call a priest?"

Morris gasped, "Maybe you would like it better if our rabbi caught smallpox?"

Rebecca was an heiress, but with a face even her accountant couldn't love. In desparation, her mamma finally suggested that they place an ad in the personal column of a leading tabloid.

It read: "Charming young heiress, money no problem, wants to live life to the fullest with man who is ready for EVERYTHING."

Surely such a come-on should bring results and mamma kept pressing Becky to let her see the responses that were supposedly pouring in.

Becky kept hedging, but at last was forced to relent.

"Only one letter came in, mamma," she admitted sadly.

"So nu, so who was it from?" mamma persisted.

Came the answer, "Daddy!"

Hymie's wife was a shrew. She never spoke to him in a normal voice, it was always a screech. One Friday he came home early and found his wife lighting the Sabbath candles and praying in a soft melodious tone. He was touched at the gentleness in her voice and awed by the beauty of the scene. He looked at her and asked, "Tillie, why don't you ever talk to me like you can talk to the candles?"

She answered, "If you would burn like the candles, I would talk to you the same way."

The waiter in the Greasy Spoon came up to the man who had just parked on a stool at the counter. "I'll have a bowl of chicken soup, please," said the diner.

"Chickenzoup!" the waiter bawled back to the kitchen.

"No, on second thought, I believe I'll have pea soup."

"Make the chicken pea!" boomed the waiter.

"Er, never mind," gulped the diner. "Maybe I'd better just have a hamburger."

Howard, who was one of New York's leading custom tailors, went to Rome for a vacation. While there, his wife, who was a firm believer in 'when in Rome do as the Romans', insisted that they have an audience with the Pope. It was arranged through the American Embassy and they were granted their audience.

When they returned to New York they told one and all of their trip and of course about the visit to the Pope. Howard's father asked, "Howard, tell me, what is the Pope really like?"

His son replied, "He's a 42 short."

One night, after a long, cold season of not any, Morris found himself inching closer and closer to Sadie's side of the bed. Suddenly, she jumped up.

"Don't touch me, you sex fiend!" she screamed.

"Sadie, Sadie, listen," Morris pleaded softly, "once every six months doesn't make me a sex fiend!"

The young mother was taking every possible precaution to insure a sanitary surrounding for her infant son. Up to the time he was four months old, visitors were required to wear surgical face masks.

One day the mother turned to the father and said:

"Alexander seems to be cutting a tooth and I suppose I should find out about it somehow."

"Well," suggested her husband, "my mother used to put her finger in the baby's mouth and . . ."

Noticing the horrified expression on his wife's face, he quickly added:

"Oh, of course, you boil the finger first."

Minnie and Sol had been married 20 years and it was their anniversary. After an evening on the town they returned home. She put on a brand new negligee; he, new satin pajamas and they got into bed.

After lying next to each other for five minutes, with nobody making a move, Minnie asked, "What's the matter, Sol, can't you think of anyone either?"

The reason there are so many Jewish dentists is because members of the dental profession are the only men who can tell a woman to open or close her mouth and get away with it.

The kid with the horn-rimmed glasses is getting a terrific tongue-lashing from his mother for using a four-letter word.

"But, Mother, he interrupts, "Tennessee Williams uses that word all the time."

And the mother answers: "Well, don't play with him then!"

Becky and Abie wanted to get a wonderful wedding gift for their daughter Shirley. Becky got a brilliant idea—if they got her a tape recorder and hid it under the bed on her wedding night, Shirley would have a record of the most marvelous night of her life. So they did, and after Shirley and her new husband went on their honeymoon, Becky and Abie played the tape. All they heard was Shirley's voice saying "Thaaat's haaapiness, thaaat's haaapiness," over and over again. "Isn't that marvelous?" said Becky with tears in her eyes.

"Dope!" said Abie, "you're playing it on the wrong speed." He fixed the speed and heard Shirley's voice saying "That's a penis? That's a penis? That's a penis?"

A man was dying. Just before he passed away, he said to his wife who was sitting by the bedside, "Darling, I have only one regret. I hate to leave you behind in all your loneliness. I just want you to know that, if you should ever remarry, you have my blessing. Only, if you do, I wonder if you would promise me something?"

"Yes, darling," his wife said. "What is it?"

"Would you promise not to let your new husband wear my old clothes and remind you of me?" he asked.

"Why, certainly I'll promise you that," his wife said. "I wouldn't think of doing such a thing. Besides, Milton doesn't like your taste in clothes."

A little boy looked at his mother's fur coat and remarked, "How that poor beast must have suffered so that you might have that coat."

His mother screamed, "Shut up, you shouldn't talk about your father that way."

The salesman had tried consistently and unsuccessfully for five years to sell a tough prospect. After each visit, the salesman grunted, "I wish I had a hundred like you." When the customer became curious and asked him why he kept repeating that phrase, the salesman replied, "I have a thousand like you, but I wish I only had a hundred!"

There are lies, damn lies, and satistics. F'rinstance, statistics say there are seven million Jews in the world, and 750 million Chinese. Well, you go down to the beach any summer Sunday, and find me one Chinaman!

Ecstatic over his new love, Dudley Cohen sat down to extoll the girl's virtue to his father. "Daddy," he rhapsodised, "I've found a girl just like Mother!"

"So what do you want," scowled his father, "sympathy?"

A harassed housewife called on a psychiatrist with this complaint: "Doctor, my husband thinks he is Moses."

The analyst suggested that she have patience and reassured her that her husband's imagining of power and greatness was only a passing phase.

"I do hope so," sighed the wife, "but in the meanwhile, how can I keep him from parting the water in the tub when I'm taking a bath?"

Louie was paying his first visit to a house of ill repute. As the girl undressed, he was dismayed to see a great growth of underarm hair.

"Oy," he wailed aloud, "so much wool, so much wool!"

As the girl disrobed completely, he saw a further, lower, even more prodigous growth. Again he exclaimed, "So much wool, so much wool!"

The hooker, angry by now, snapped at him, "Listen mister, did you come here to screw —or to knit?"

YENTA 8

Harry had to drive his wife and mother-in-law from Brooklyn to the Catskills and all along the way the two women in his life were giving him advice on how to drive.

Finally Harry couldn't take it any more and pulled the car to the side of the road and furiously turned to his wife in the back seat and whined, "All right. Now let's get this straight once and for all. Who's driving this car. You...or your mother?"

Polly Adler always averred that hers was the best business of all: you got it, you sell it, you still got it!

This is about a family that went picnicking on a Sunday. They found a lovely spot in the country, spread out the tablecloth and covered it with sandwiches, hard-boiled eggs, etc. Impressed by the beauty of the place, they were puzzled by the flags with numbers they saw at various points in the distance.

Midway through their picnic, a man strode angrily toward them. "Just what do you think you are doing?" he exploded. "Don't you realize you are sitting on the fifteenth green of the most exclusive golf club in the country?"

Papa swallowed his hardboiled egg and sarcastically answered, "So, is this the way to get new members?"

1st man: I went hunting in Africa and I bagged a lion.
2nd man: You bagged a lion?
1st man: Sure, I bagged him and bagged him he should please go away!

Max was the owner of a famous delicatessen, and being a very charitable human being, never turns down a panhandler. He just doesn't give them a sandwich. He gives them fifty cents, tells them to sit at a table, order something and pay for it like a respectable customer. It has double value. He gets the money back and it helps instill self-respect in the bum. One night, in came a panhandler. Max, seeing the terrible night out, decided to give more than usual, seventy five cents, and told him to go to a table and order.

The fellow sat down, looked at the menu and started a commotion. Max rushed over and asked what was wrong.

"Listen," bellowed the bum, "where in hell do you come to get sixty cents for a salami sandwich!"

Two women were talking. One said to the other, "That Rose is always knocking her husband. I never heard anything like it in my whole life. She's always complaining about him...look at my husband, he's such a louse he should drop dead, but do I ever say anything to anybody?"

Two refugee women were talking about their children and how well they had done in the United States. "How does your daughter like America?" the first one asked.

"Wonderful," the woman said. "She married an American boy. He helps her with the house, he washes the dishes, he stays with the baby when she wants to go out. He does everything for her. And how is your son doing?"

"Oh, the poor boy. It is terrible," she said. "He married an American girl. He has to help her with the house, and wash the dishes, and stay with the baby when she wants to go out. Everything, he has to do!"

After having their third child Irving decided to ask the family doctor how to avoid having any more children. The doctor took out a box and told him, "Be sure to put one of these on your organ before you make love to your wife and I promise that you won't have any more children."

Three months later Irving and Fanny were back and after examing her the doctor announced that she was going to have another baby. He asked Irving why he hadn't used what he gave him. Irving answered he had used the whole box, but, since they didn't have an organ he had put them on the piano.

The smallest book in the world: "The Complete Guide to Jewish Business Ethics".

Seymour and Sammy had been partners in a dress manufacturing business for years. Their relationship, in and out of the shop, had been cordial.

Sammy lived on the West Side in Manhattan and Seymour in Brooklyn. Seymour's doctor thought he looked overly tired and suggested he move into Manhattan nearer to the business. His friend, Sammy, located an apartment for him a few blocks from his house.

A few weeks later, on Yom Kippur, Seymour was walking to the synagogue, as was his custom, to attend services. On the way, he passed a sea-food restaurant. He casually glanced in and was shocked to see his partner, Sammy, sitting at a table near the window eating oysters!

He couldn't contain himself! He rushed in and with a voice quivering with emotion, blurted out, "Sammy, my partner and pal for thirty years! I can't believe my eyes! Not only are you not in the synagogue and fasting, but you're eating oysters yet!"

"So what's to get excited, Seymour?" said Sammy calmly. "What's the matter, there's no 'R' in Yom Kippur?"

Father to son: How dare you disobey your mother! Do you think you're better than I am?

"My boy," said the magnate to his son, "there are two things that are vitally necessary if you are to succeed in business."

"What are they, dad?"

"Honesty and sagacity."

"What is honesty?"

"Always—no matter what happens or how adversely it may affect you—always keep your word once you have given it."

"And sagacity?"

"Never give it."

Sandra was hanging up her husband Steve's jacket when she noticed a long grey hair on the shoulder.

"So," she screamed at him, "you've been over at your mother's getting sympathy again!"

A minister, a priest and a rabbi were discussing how they "divined" what part of the collection money each retained for personal needs and what part was turned in to their respective institutions.

"I draw a line," said the minister, "on the floor. All the money I toss in the air—what lands to the right of the line I keep, to the left of the line is the Lord's."

The priest nodded, saying "My system is essentially the same, only I use a circle. What lands inside is mine, outside His."

The rabbi smiled and said, "I do the same thing. I toss all the money into the air and whatever God grabs, is His!"

During the darkest period of early World War II, a Jewish financier received an audience with King George of England.

The King was despondent.

"London is being raided nightly," he lamented. "Rommel may capture Suez, India is in ferment and Japan menaces Australia. What can I do?"

The banker pondered, and finally spoke: "Your Majesty," he suggested, "if I were you, I'd put Canada in the Queen's name!"

What's the difference between a Polack, an Englishman, and a Jew?

When coming off an airplane, the Polack walks off without even looking to see if he left anything behind; the Englishman walks off after looking back to see if he has left anything behind; the Jew waits around to see whether anybody else has left anything behind.

Some husbands maintain they deserve at least one night off each week. Mr. Finkelstein was one of these and what's more, he convinced Mrs. Finkelstein of the merit of his position. So every Friday, regular as clockwork, he would hop into his car and join the boys at the local bar for a drink or two. One day he didn't come home and he was gone for seven years. Then, one Friday evening, he returned as suddenly as he had disappeared.

Mrs. Finkelstein was so happy to see him, that she called up all her friends to come and celebrate.

"Wait just a minute," objected Mr. Finkelstein. "What do you think you're doing?"

"Just having a few friends over in honor of your return," said Mrs. Finkelstein.

"What?" growled Finkelstein. "On my night out?"

Hymie Mandelbaum had reached the glorious age of 92 with very little medical difficulties. Feeling sort of under the weather, he went to see a doctor. After making some preliminary tests, the medic informed his patient, "You either have V.D. or the measles. I'll make a few more tests and let you know for sure." Mandelbaum waited patiently.

The doctor returned to the office and announced, "Well, Mr. Mandelbaum, I'm afraid it's V.D."

"Naturally," smiled the oldster, "where would I come in contact with measles?"

Every man to his own trade. When it was announced that his wife gave birth to a 12 pound child, a proud father ran around the neighborhood telling all the good news. Into Sam the butcher he rushed and yelled: "I got a boy, a twelve pound boy!"

"Including the bones?" asked Sam.

Three little boys were playing on the street in Birmingham, Alabama. Two of the little boys turned to the third child and said, "We can't play with you any more."

"Why not?" asked the child, in dismay.

"Because you're Jewish," answered the two other little boys.

The little Jewish boy looked at them and replied, "But we're not playing for money."

Two old cronies met on the street and, naturally, started exchanging grievances.

"Oy," said Simon, "that son of mine will be my ruination. All he does all day long is run around the showroom chasing the models."

"So," answered Sol, "you think you got troubles? My son is even more of a problem. He's also all day after the models."

Demanded Simon, "Is it worse with your son than with mine?"

Sol sighed, "Simon, Simon, you forget—I'm in men's wear."

In Miami Beach everybody is rich, even the poor people. One woman has a cashmere car and mink dental floss. One day I went to the hotel pool to get an estimate on a swim.

Sam Silverstein, a successful dress manu-facturer, had to make a trip to the West Coast on business. Sadie, his loving wife, resented it bitterly because it meant cele-brating their anniversary alone. Plead as she would, Sam couldn't avoid the trip and left tearful Sadie behind. Every night he called from the Coast and every conversa-tion ended with pain and sobs.

Sam had to do something special to prove his own great anguish and love, so one eve-ning he phoned and said, "Sadie dear, I'm sending you two wonderful presents — a Picasso and a Jaguar."

A few days later, Sam asked Sadie during one of their phone conversations, "Didn't the Picasso and the Jaguar arrive yet?"

"Not both, Sam," answered Sadie sadly, "only one of them came."

"Good! Wonderful!" Sam exclaimed. "Which one?"

"Who knows?" answered Sadie.

A Texan walked into a bar with an alligator under his arm. He walked up to the bar-tender and shouted, "Do you serve Jews in this bar?" The bartender decided that the best way to handle him was to say yes. The Texan replied, "Give me a scotch and soda and give my alligator a Jew."

A businessman called all his creditors together to give them the jolly news that he was going into bankruptcy.

"All together, I owe you guys over two hundred thousand dollars," he told them. "Unfortunately, my assets won't cover a payment of five cents on a dollar, so I guess you won't be able to get anything—unless you would like to cut me up and divide me among you."

One of the creditors spoke up, "I move we do it. I'd like to have his gall."

Menachem, an ultra-orthodox Jew, had a son who was drafted into the army. To make sure that everything was as it should be, Menachem gathered himself together and set off on the long train trip to rural Georgia. Dressed in his long frock coat, yarlmeka, curly earlocks dancing in the wind, he was quite a sight to the gawking townspeople as he descended from the train.

To his annoyance, Menachem discovered he was being trailed by a passel of kids, mimicing him as he walked. Suddenly, the old man turned to them and shouted angrily, "What's the matter? Ain't you ever seen a Yankee before?"

A guest at a mountain health resort flatly refused to follow the prescribed schedule of set-up exercises and work-outs.

"I came here to eat and to rest," he insisted. "Exercise is to me not necessary."

When he was checking out, the proprietor pleaded:

"Before you leave, just do one bit of exercise for me—to keep my record clear. Please just bend down, keep your knees straight, and touch your valise."

The man Bent over and said, "Well, I'm touching. What now?"

"Open it," said the proprietor, "and give me back my towels."

"Business sure is off," complained Isaac Gottlieb, the biggest mortician in town. His friend looked puzzled.

"All four of these caskets are occupied," he said, "so how bad can things be?"

Just then two of the corpses sat up and Gottlieb's buddy turned ashen. "Take it easy, Morris," Gottlieb quickly explained, "they're just my partners trying to make the place look busy."

A Martian lands in Levittown, sees a man watering his lawn and says: "Take me to your leader!" And the man answers: "I can't. She's in Monticello with the kids."

For their 17th wedding anniversary Morris bought Zelda a family plot. On the approach of their 18th wedding anniversary, Zelda asked Morris, "What are you going to give me this year for our anniversary?"

He replied, "Nothing. You still didn't use what I gave you last year."

A couple from the Bronx and their four children were downtown and decided to take a taxi home. Approaching the cab driver the husband demanded, "How much will you charge to drive us to the Bronx?"

"I figure two dollars apiece for you and your wife," said the driver, "and I'll take the four kids for nothin'."

The husband turned to his kids and said, "Jump in, children, and have a nice ride home. Mamma and I will take the subway."

Stanley, well-known man-about-town and bon vivant, ran into a church hurriedly. Dashing into the confession booth, he exploded, "Father, Father, I just made love to a woman twenty-five times!"

Asked the priest, "Are you married?"

Stanley answered, 'No, and I'm Jewish, not Catholic, but I had to tell someone!"

Psychiatrist: A Jewish doctor who can't stand the sight of blood.

Goldstein, who lives in the city most of the year but summers in Maine, was surprised one winter day when he received a call from the caretaker of his summer place.

"There's a bad forest fire up here," he was informed, "and it looks like your house might get burned down."

My goodness!" the homeowner exclaimed. "Is there anything I can do?"

"Well," the down-easter replied, "I thought maybe you might want to put more insurance on it."

A man called his partner from Miami and said, "Sam, this is Max, how's everything in New York?"

Sam: Very good.

Max: How's the weather up there?

Sam: The weather's how it should be.

Max: How's business in the shop?

Sam: Very good, but I got bad news for you.

Max: What's the matter?

Sam: We've been robbed.

Max: Don't be silly, PUT IT BACK!

One of the greatest puzzles is how the boy who wasn't good enough to marry the daughter can become the father of the smartest grandchildren in the world.

Bridgehampton Schwartz, fabulous wheeler-dealer and entrepeneur internationale, got a very important phone call from his real estate broker. "Bridge baby, I got good news and bad news for you on that Florida hotel deal."

"So," said Schwartz, "so tell me."

"Well, first the good news," said the broker. "Instead of the five million bucks they had asked for, they'll sell for three and a half."

"So, nu, good," sighed Schwartz, "what then?"

"Well, the bad news," said the broker, "they want two thousand down in cash."

Then there was the chap who went to a quiet farmhouse to get a rest and fell into a half filled cesspool on his first night walk over the grounds.

"Help!" he shouted, "Fire! Fire!"

In a short time the fireman, policeman and all the other guests arrived and dragged him besmirched and forlorn from the smelly pit.

"What's the idea of yelling 'Fire'?" demanded the chief. "There's no fire here."

"What did you want me to holler?" answered the irate guest. "Crap?"

A woman came before the local judge complaining that her husband had made a murderous attack on her with a large pair of scissors.

"Judge," she cried, "he rushed at me and slashed my face to pieces!"

The judge looked at her face, on which not the slightest mark of conflict appeared.

"When did you say this happened?"

"Only last night, Judge."

"But I don't see any marks on your face," said the puzzled judge.

"Marks!" roared the woman. "What do I care about marks? I've got witnesses!"

Samuel Seigal, the famous professor of law, was lecturing on courtroom procedure. "When you're fighting a case," he said, "if you have the facts on your side, hammer on the facts. If you have the law on your side, hammer on the law."

"But if you don't have the facts or the law," asked a student, "what do you do?"

"In that case," the professor said, "then hammer on the table."

It was Christmas Eve and a couple were coming home from the midnight service. The wife spotted their Jewish neighbors and said, "Look, dear, what a beautiful scene. The Millers are carrying in a Yule log."

"That's no Yule log," her husband replied. "That's Miller."

Mrs. Lapidus was shopping at a super-market and went to the meat department to purchase a chicken. The butcher selected one from the refrigerator and extended it toward Mrs. Lapidus for her approval.

The fastidious Mrs. Lapidus grasped the fowl by its neck and brought it up close for inspection. She lifted a wing and sniffed there, then lifted the other wing and smelled that. Then, she turned the chicken about and sniffed the part that goes over the fence last. She then handed it back to the butcher, made a face and said, "It stinks!"

The butcher studied her for a moment, and asked:

"Madam, do you think YOU could pass such a test?"

A rather well-dressed man called on a rabbi and told him a distressing story of poverty and misery in the neighborhood.

"This poor widow," he said, "with four starving children to feed, is sick in bed with no money for the doctor, and besides that she owes $100 rent for three months and is about to be evicted. I'm out trying to help raise the rent money. I wondered if you can help?"

"I certainly can," said the rabbi, "if you can give your time to this cause, so can I. By the way, who are you?"

"I'm the landlord," the man said.

An extremely attractive model appeared to be perfect choice to display the manufac-turer's new spring line.

"Yes, you're just what we need," he told her. "You have the right face, the right fig-ure, everything is right. By the way, how much do you expect a week?"

The girl told him the amount.

"Sorry," said the boss quickly, "you're too tall!"

All his life Herman had slaved in his little store to earn enough to make something of his only son. When he thought the boy showed promise as a musician, he scraped together every cent he could lay his hands on and sent him to Europe to study with the finest teachers.

Ten years went by and the boy finally sent a telegram home that he was ready to return. Overjoyed, Herman rented Carnegie Hall, gave tickets to all his friends, relatives and customers, and announced that after the concert there would be a huge banquet—if the boy was a success. Came the night of the big event, the son sauntered on stage with his shirt hanging out, his collar hanging out, his strings hanging out. In short, a fiasco.

Herman was crushed but not too badly to remember to cancel the feast. He rushed over to the hotel only to find two relatives already seated in the ballroom and stuffing their faces.

"Didn't I tell you there'd be a dinner only if the boy were a success!" shrieked Herman.

"So?" shrugged the relatives, "We liked him!"

Two guys went to school to study economics. They went into partnership and opened a store. They failed in 3 months. A fellow who had no schooling bought the place from them, and was a big success. The former partners talked to him: "We studied economy and failed in business. You bought the store from us and are a success—how do you do it?"

"I'll tell you. I'm a very plain businessman. I buy a thing for a dollar and sell it for two dollars—I'm satisfied with my one per cent profit."

Now that Mrs. Nussbaum was in the money, she had to have the same or better than her neighbors in the way of furnishings. She went to the city's leading antique store and in her ritziest manner commanded: "I want to see some period furniture!"

The clerk bowed humbly and asked, "Do you wish to see period examples of Early American, Old English or French Empire?"

"No," she replied, "I want the kind that when the neighbors see it, they should drop dead—PERIOD!"

Frazier Fenster, senior partner in the well-known Wall Street brokerage house of Meyer, Lind, Pearl, Fenster and Bein, was seventy-four and seriously ill. An old friend visited him.

"Frazier, you shouldn't worry. Wait yet, you'll see, God will let you live yet, you'll go to eighty!"

Fenster snarled, "What do you think, God is a fool? If He can get me at 74, why should he wait till I hit 80?"

Business had been worse than terrible all year, but Weiner, the owner, grimly went ahead with the annual year-end employee party. After dinnner had been served, he rose to make his customary address.

"My dear friends," he intoned, "I won't bore you with a long speech. We're out of business. Thank you and good-night."

Becky was walking down Main Street when she bumped into her next door neighbor, Sadie. She asked Sadie where she was going in such a rush. Sadie answered, "Congratulate me. My daughter Jeanette just gave birth to a baby boy."

Becky looked at her with a smirk, "How come, she is only married five months?"

Sadie stared at her and replied, "My Jeanette is such a young innocent girl, she knows how long to carry?"

When the waiter brought the check, Bernstein asked, "What's this five dollars for?"

The waiter, typical of the Jewish delicatessen type, answered condescendingly, "That's for your chopped liver sandwich."

Bernstein screamed, "Who's liver was it—Rockefeller's?"

Joe Bloom had made a fortune in the garment industry and decided to send his one and only daughter to the finest European boarding schools to give her "Culture." After being away at school for two years, the girl wired her father that she wanted to return home immediately.

When she entered his house he was speechless at her poise and breeding. She was truly a lady to her fingertips. When she spoke, her speech was flawless. After studying the effect she had on her father for a few moments, the girl finally looked at him long and hard and said, "Father, before we say another word to each other, I feel that you should know that I am in trouble and expect to have a baby."

Her father, shocked, turned to the girl and asked, "Who is the responsible party?"

His daughter looked at him and replied, "I know this will be hard to believe, but, I never took the time to find out his name."

The father looked at the girl and shouted, "Do you mean to tell me that with all your fancy schooling they never taught you to even ask, "With whom am I having the pleasure?"

Two men were chatting, when the name of a mutual friend was mentioned. "Are you a friend of Harry's?" the first asked.

"Are we friends?" the man said. "Twenty years we're friends. There's nothing I wouldn't do for Harry and there's nothing he wouldn't do for me. In fact, for twenty years, we've gone through life together, doing absolutely nothing for each other."

The renting agent in a brand new luxury apartment house on the East Side was pointing out the various features of an apartment. The prospective tenant, Mr. Krentzel, agreed that the apartment was attractive but he hesitated because the building seemed flimsily constructed, and not too steady.

"What do you expect?" retorted the agent, "The wall paper isn't up yet!"

"Shiksa"—woman who does her own housework.

Yossel was from a small town near Vilna, and he finally saved up enough to pay his passage to America. The fourth day out at sea, a terrific storm broke out. Excitement and fear raged on board ship. The captain shouted orders through a megaphone. Sailors lowered lifeboats, women screamed, children cried, dogs barked, while everyone else milled about the ship in great confusion. Only Yossel remained tranquil and detached from the whole scene.

"How can you be so unconcerned when the whole ship is sinking?" screamed a fellow passenger at the smiling Yossel.

"What are you so excited about?" asked the little immigrant. "Does the ship belong maybe to you?"

Sign on Marcus' tailor shop:
WE'LL CLEAN FOR YOU. WE'LL PRESS FOR YOU. WE'LL EVEN DYE FOR YOU.

Bernice Gladstone became a widow quite sudden-like and was left a cool million dollars. Several months passed and she became very morose, going about weeping. Her friends tried to console her with the fact that she now had a million bucks, and that she should go out and enjoy herself.

"That's what you think," she wailed, "right now, I'd give ten thousand dollars of it, just to have him back!"

The operation had just been completed and the surgeon was washing up. He was joined by one of the young interns who inquired, "How did Mrs. Shoenfeld's appendectomy go?"

"Appendectomy?" shrieked the surgeon, "I thought it was an autopsy!"

Hilda and Leon were sitting on the lawn of a posh resort, enjoying themselves. At least, Hilda was. "Listen to those gorgeous little birds sing," she chortled. "They sound so happy!"

"Why shouldn't they be happy?" grumbled her husband, "it isn't costing them eighty dollars a day!"

An attorney, Murray Schwartz, was constantly annoyed at dinner parties when guests asked him for free legal advice. He asked a doctor friend if he had the same experiences.

"Oh, yes," replied the doctor.

"How do you squelch them?"

"I discovered a perfect method," the doctor answered. "When they begin to describe their ailments, I ask them to undress!"

Moe met his friend Sol on the street. He looked at Sol and said, "Sol, I haven't seen you in three years. You look terrible. What has been happening to you?"

Sol answered, "Moe, don't ask. Would you believe I got married three times in the last three years and buried three wives?"

Moe said, "How tragic, what happened?"

Sol replied, "Well, three years ago I married this wonderful girl and she died a month later after eating poisoned mushrooms. A year later, I met this lovely girl and she died a month after we were married after eating poisoned mushrooms. Then last year I married again and believe it or not, after one month she died."

Moe said, "Don't tell me, poisoned mushrooms?"

"No fractured skull. She wouldn't eat the poisoned mushrooms."

A wife called up a friend and said delightedly: "Am I lucky! My husband had a nervous breakdown, so now we have to go to Florida for the winter!"

The tower bell at the Vatican stopped working. Bell repairmen were sent for from all parts of the world to fix the bell, to no avail. After months of searching, a bell repairman was found in Israel and he agreed to fly to Rome and fix the bill for a nominal fee. After months of silence, all of Rome was informed that the bell was fixed and would peal once again at 7:00 A.M. on Sunday. The crowds gathered and a hush fell over the city as the hour approached and then the bell began to peal, "Goyim! Goyim! Goyim!"

Two litigants were getting a bit hot under the collar.
Moskowitz: "I'll sue you in the state court!"
Margolis: "I'll meet you there!"
Moskowitz: "I'll sue you in the Supreme Court!"
Margolis: "I'll be there to answer you!"
Moskowitz: "I'll sue you to the deepest level of hell!"
Margolis: "My attorney will be there!"

Goldwynism: Sam, on being told his latest actress discovery had very beautiful hands: "Yes, very beautiful hands. I'm thinking of having a bust made of them."

"Sidney, if your father earned $240 a week and gave your mother half, what would she have?"
"Heart failure."

Miss Greenberg was teaching her English class when she asked the class if any one of the children could make a sentence out of th words 'commercial' and 'official'.
Little Irving waved his hand at once and said, "That's easy, Miss Greenberg. My mother said to my brother, 'Come Moishel, eat a fishel'."

The father, who had been approached by his daughter's fiance, told the young man, "I see no reason why you shouldn't marry my daughter—can you support a family?"
"I'm prepared to do that, sir."
"Good," replied the old man, holding out his hand. "Counting my daughter, there are seven of us."

"How is your husband getting along after his accident?"
"His doctor says he can walk around again, but his lawyer says he can't."

Jake went on his first trip for his firm. He checked into his hotel and was just about to go up to his room, when a blonde walked over to him and said, "You don't know me and I don't know you, but you just got the last room in the hotel. Since you don't know me and I don't know you, do you think I could spend the night in your room?"

He looked at her and shrugged, "I guess it would be okay." When they got to the room, he offered the girl the couch to sleep on and got into bed.

He was just about to fall asleep, when the girl came over to him and said, "You don't know me and I don't know you, but it's very cold on the couch and uncomfortable, maybe I could get into bed with you?"

He was at a loss for words and replied, "Okay."

The girl got into bed with him and the next thing he knew she whispered, "I don't know you and you don't know me, but let's have a party."

He looked at her and replied, "Ordinarily it would be fun, but, since you don't know me and I don't know you, who would we invite to a party?"

Overheard at a Hadassah meeting: "OK, so I like to spend money. Name one other extravagance."

As Grandma Cohen approached her ninetieth birthday, her family, now all successful, made plans for a gala celebration. They asked what she wanted for a present, and promised to make her wish come true, no matter what it was. But there was nothing Grandma wanted—except to sit.

"How about a ride in an airplane?" suggested one publicity-conscious relative. "I could arrange the flight."

"I ain't ridin' in no new flyin' machine," said the determined old lady who had crossed the Atlantic in steerage. "I'll just sit here and watch television, like God intended I should."

Morris Mishkin was a highly successful dairy farmer in Tom's River, New Jersey. He came to the attention of cattle breeders all over the country when he mated a Golden Guernsey with a Holstein, and so created a new breed, the Goldstein. This is the remarkable animal that says "Nu" instead of "Moo," and incidently, if you should ever get one for cooking purposes, the meat is already kosher.

Everybody comes to Sam's delicatessen... everybody, that is, but the Health Inspector.

"Law offices of Cohen, Goldfarb, Cohen, and O'Hare."

"How did O'Hare get in there?"

"He put up the money."

Rosalie Mazzolli, nee Adelstein, had married a midget. For a while, they were getting along all right, but one day Rosalie showed up in domestic relations court, and demanded she be granted a divorce from little Harry.

"Surely, Mrs. Mazzolli, you knew your husband was a midget when you married him," questioned the judge, "why are you now desirous of leaving him? Didn't you anticipate the problems this marriage would encounter?"

"Oh, your honor," sobbed Rosalie, "how was I to know? Everything is wonderful, except for sex."

"Sex?" repeated the judge, "what has his being a midget got to do with sex?"

"Well," she continued tearfully, "when we're nose to nose, his toes are in it, when we're toes to nose, his nose is in it, and when he's in it, he disappears altogether, and oh, your honor, I get so lonely!"

Soon as Judge Hirschman sentenced the bookie to prison for 20 years, he rushed away from the bench and out of the court, to which an attendant asked: "You aren't afraid of him, are you, Judge?"

"No, I'm going over to rent his apartment."

A beggar knocked on the door of a house and begged the woman of the house for something to eat. He told her that he hadn't eaten in three days. She looked at him and said, "Shame on you. A big strong husky-looking galoot like you begging."

He sighed, "Lady, isn't bad enough I have to be a beggar, do I have to be a cripple too?"

The stewardess on the Israel airlines comes over the loudspeaker and says—"Your stewardesses are Mrs. Rose Bergman and Mrs. Fanny Klein and, of course, my son, the pilot."

Applebaum's analyst pinpointed the problem:
Applebaum wanted to get back into the womb—anybody's!

Tessie had worked very hard all her life to provide her children with the very best possible. To her utter dismay, her youngest daughter, her Rosalie, at the age of sixteen, was turning into a regular beatnik, and growing further and further from the simple, traditional teachings of her mother. Tessie still held out hope for her beloved youngest, and continued to pamper and indulge the girl.

Rosalie had run through her allowance and was explaining this to her mother as best she could. Finally Tessie sighed, "All right, darling. You need a couple dollars, I'll give you. But sweetheart, on Passover you don't say, 'Lay a little bread on me!'."

A father sent his little son Scott to the Temple's Sunday school for the first time. After a month the parent called up the Sunday school teacher to find out how the boy was doing.

"I'm teaching him the prayer for the dead."

"What," yelped the father, "you're teaching him the prayer for the dead? Am I dying, or is my wife dying that you should teach him the prayer for the dead?"

"Listen," replied the teacher, "you should live so long till he'll learn it!"

"Sammy, come down, do you hear? Come down or you'll break your legs. Sammy, Momma's telling you! All right, Sammy, but when you fall down and break both legs, don't come running to **me!**"

Henry Horowitz, the cloth converter, (mostly he converted the cloth into money!), decided to send his son Sheldon to Europe for a few months as the boy was completely useless in business. In Europe, with luck, his father figured, he may even pick up a little bit of culture and henceforward could be considered artistic, to explain his lack of business ability.

After six months' dalliance, Sheldon cabled he was coming home. His mother and father were astonished to see he had a big, blowsy-looking blonde in tow. He carefully guided the cow-like creature over to where his parents were waiting.

"Mom, Dad," he announced proudly, "I want you to meet your new daughter-in-law!" He spoke to her in some gibberish and the blonde nodded sleepily.

"What!" his father screamed, "this you call a wife? This is what you bring us after all this time and not to mention money spent? This cow?"

"Dad," the son tried to explain, "she's no ordinary girl. Ursula is a baroness!"

"What!" roared his father, turning purple. "You mean she can't even have children?"

Mr. and Mrs. Davidowitz were having a violent quarrel, and the husband was losing control of his temper.

"Be careful," he warned, "you'll bring out the beast in me."

"So what!" she countered. "Who's afraid of mice?"

Irving was a talent agent. It being the year of the two big singing sensations, the Singing Nun and the Beatles, he decided to create the greatest act of all by combining the two, which he called the "Praying Mantis".

Old man Levine brought a package to the post office but the clerk refused to accept it.

"What's the matter?"

"It's too heavy; you'll have to put more stamps on it."

"And if I put more stamps on it that will make it lighter?"

A successful cloak-and-suiter had finally found the girl of his dreams and he made preparations for a wedding the garment district would never forget. His own designers prepared a wedding gown for the bride of the finest imported silks and satins, and his own marital raiment was truly a sight to behold.

The affair was nothing less than breathtaking. No expense had been spared. Then, as the newly-weds were about to embark on their honeymoon trip to Canada, an urgent message arrived in the form of a telegram.

"It's from my partner," the groom explained. "Urgent business. I'll have to attend to it immediately."

"But what about our honeymoon?" the bride asked tearfully.

"Business comes first," he said. "But you go ahead. I'll catch a later plane and be there by tonight."

"But what if you can't make it by tonight?" she moaned.

"Then—" he blustered, "start without me."

So who needs a friend at Chase Manhattan? At another New York bank, the Irving Trust Company, you have family!

Ikey asked his mother if he could watch a solar eclipse.

"Okay," she replied, "but don't go too close."

Mrs. Cohen met Mrs. Goldberg and asked how her son was, to which Mrs. Goldberg replied, "Good and bad." Mrs. Cohen asked for an explanation.

Mrs. Goldberg explained that her son had run off to live with a man, which was bad; however, the man was a doctor, which was good.

Did you hear about the new discotheque that opened in Israel? It's called Let My People Go Go.

The woman listened carefully as the doctor prescribed a remedy for her nervous condition. "Lady," he said, "you need frequent baths, plenty of fresh air, and you should dress in warm clothes." That night after supper she told her husband about it.
"The doctor," she said, "told me I am in a highly nervous condition, and that I must go to Miami Beach, then to a dude ranch out west, and buy myself a full-length mink coat."

A panhandler knocked at Mrs. Stein's back door. "Please ma'am," he asked, tattered hat in hand, "could I have some of yesterday's soup?"
"Yesterday's soup?" the stylish stout repeated, "certainly, young man, come back tomorrow."

Mollie was always a ray of sunshine, but they fired her from her job in the sanitary napkin factory when she was caught putting get-well cards in each box.

Beauregard Buchsbaum, the ladies' lingerie king, was showing a group of customers the glassed-in garden on his enormous terrace. One sweet little assistant buyer remarked on a singularly exotic looking bloom and asked her host what kind of flower it was.
Replied Buchsbaum suavely, "How should I know, sweetheart? Am I in millinery?"

"You say this fellow Gittleson is crooked?"
"Is he crooked? Say, he's so crooked even the wool he pulls over your eyes is half cotton!"

He was an unsuccessful politician, poor but dishonest. He went to his ward leader. "I have thirty votes in my family and I control two hundred more. Why can't I be assemblyman?"

After a little persuasion, the leader ran him for office and he was elected. Two years later he was back again requesting to be made a congressman. The leader granted this request, too, and he was elected. Four years later he asked to be run for governor. Again the leader consented and again he won.

Soon he was back again and said to the boss, "You must do me another favor."

"What now?" screamed the head politician. "I made you an assemblyman, I made you a congressman and I made you a governor. What do you want me to do now! Make you the President?"

"No," whimpered the Governor, "make me a citizen."

Two partners with a small store down a side street in a poor neighborhood were going broke.

"I think we'd better quit the store," the first one said. "Business is terrible. We haven't made a dime in a whole month. I think we ought to close up and look for a job."

"I can't understand it," said the other. "We're not doing any business at all, and here in the paper, the President says business is wonderful!"

"Well," said his partner, "maybe he's got a better location."

"I saw a man-eating shark at the aquarium."

"So nu? I saw a man eating herring in the park."

Two Jews were walking along the pier when one suddenly fell in. A policeman, seeing what happened, jumped in and saved the man.

The little Jew's friend said, "He saved your life, shouldn't we give him a dollar?"

"I was half dead when he rescued me, give him 50¢."

The wife lay dying and her husband was breaking up emotionally. "Please, sweetheart, don't die. Remember, it took me a year to buy you the right kind of a mink coat, wholesale. Please, baby, if you'll live, I'll buy you a dozen times as much jewelry, wholesale!" sobbed the husband.

"So all right already, dear," spoke the wife faintly, "I'll try my best not to die. But if I should die, make me a promise . . . bury me retail."

An upstate hotel received a reservation request for next season from a Brooklynite who wrote: "Please reserve a suitable room where I can put up with my wife."

Helen Klein, who was vacationing at Miami Beach, opened her mail, glanced at a small piece of paper, stuck it back in the envelope and said to her friend who was with her, "Well, my husband is feeling good, things are going well at the office, there isn't any trouble with the cat or dog at home, and he still loves me."

"My," said her friend, "do you mean to say he told you all that on that tiny piece of paper and you read it in less than two seconds?"

"Yes," said Mrs. Klein. "It's a check for $300."

A little Jewish boy was hit by a car and was lying in the street. He had a concussion, ten broken ribs, two broken arms, and a broken leg. His mother ran down from the house to where the boy was lying, knelt down beside him, whispered some comforting words in his ear, and gave him something. What did she give him?

An enema.

Two middle-aged Jewish women were walking by the cemetery. One turned to the other and said, "That's where my daughter lays. She should only drop dead."

Mrs. Cantor suspected her husband of playing around with the maid.

Having to spend a few days with her sick mother, she told her small son, Harvey, to keep an eye on poppa and the maid.

As soon as she returned, she asked: "Harvey, did anything happen?"

"Well," said the boy, "poppa and the maid went into the bedroom and took off their clothes and—"

"Stop! Stop!" shouted Mrs. Cantor. "We will wait until poppa comes home."

Poppa was met at the door by his irate wife, cringing maid and confused son. "Harvey, tell me what happened with poppa and the maid," stormed Mrs. Cantor.

"As I told you, ma," said Harvey. "Poppa and the maid went into the bedroom and took off their clothes."

"Yes! Yes! Go on, Harvey," said Mrs. Cantor impatiently, "what did they do then?"

Replied Harvey—"Why, mother, they did the same thing you and uncle Bernie did when poppa was in Chicago."

No matter how bad her husband's business was, she kept buying and buying. After a bad day in the stock market, he came home broken; but that didn't stop her from flaunting a new, expensive gown she bought that day. He berated her for her extravagance under the conditions, but it didn't stop her. She cooed and asked: "Regardless of all that, darling, what do you really think of this gown?"

"I'll say this for you," he moaned, "you'll be the best dressed woman in the breadline!"

In old Russia it was a known fact that when the Cossacks became drunk they would attack Jewish homes and rape the women. One night, during a wild pogrom, they entered a house and found a young 16-year-old girl, her beautiful 36-year-old mother, a young looking 52-year-old grandmother, and the great-grandmother who was a toothless hag in her eighties. They each picked a woman to attack, leaving the great-grandmother out in the cold.

The old lady, learning that no one wanted her, started to yell, "That isn't fair, a pogrom is a pogrom."

A little old man was sitting on a bus humming, "Dee dee dum dum dee dee dum." The bus driver turned around and noticed a suitcase blocking the aisle. He turned to the old man and said, "Would you mind moving the suitcase?" To which the old man replied, "Dee dee dum dum, dee dee dum." In complete frustration, the bus driver jumped up and took the suitcase and threw it out the bus window and glared at the old man and shouted, "Now what do you have to say?" The old man looked at him and smiled, "Dee dee dum dum, dee, dee dum, it's not my suitcase."

While walking in the cemetery, Sol saw a man standing over a grave and crying hysterically, "Why did you die? Why did you die?" Being a Good Samaritan type, he decided to try to comfort the man and walked over. Observing the inscription on the tombstone, and seeing that it was another man's grave, he said, "I'm awfully sorry to see you so upset; this man must have been very close to you."

The man stopped crying for a minute and answered, "I never even saw him. It's my wife's first husband."

Sol had a very rare disease and the doctor told him that the only cure would be if he were castrated. Sol became hysterical and the doctor looked at him in amazement since he knew he was in his eighties and life was but a dream. He asked him, "Why should you feel so upset? You don't even really need them any more."

Sol answered, "True, but they look so sporty in the locker room."

A plane was just about to take off from Kennedy Airport. The pilot picked up the speaker and announced. "Welcome aboard T.W.A. Flight 509. Please fasten your safety belts and leave them fastened until you receive the signal to unfasten them. We will be flying at an altitude of 5,000 feet and expect to reach Miami in 2½ hours."

The pilot flicked the switch on the loudspeaker, but, it didn't go completely off and he (not realizing he was still on the air) turned to his co-pilot and said, "Boy, what I wouldn't give for a hot cup of coffee and a piece of ass." The stewardess, who was in the back of the plane, hearing this realized that the pilot didn't know that he was still on the loudspeaker, and could be heard, started to run up the aisle to tell him.

A little old lady passenger grabbed her arm, as she ran by, and said, "Sweetheart, listen to me. If I were you, I would let him finish his coffee first."

A Texan went to Israel and saw one of the small farms. He said to the Israeli farmer, "Is this your whole farm?"

When the Israeli replied in the affirmative the Texan said, "Why, back in Texas, I get in my car at five in the morning, and I drive and I drive and I drive, and at dusk I just reach the other side of my ranch."

The Israeli thought for a while, and then replied, "I used to have a car like that."

Mr. Finesilver was skipping along the street humming a gay tune. His neighbor, falling in step with him, remarked, "You're pretty happy this morning."

"Right you are," grinned Finesilver. "I just cured my wife of yelling at me all the time."

"Well, well. How did you do it?"

"I convinced her it was making a nervous wreck out of the French poodle."

A man visited an analyst because he thought he was Colonel Nasser. The headshrinker assured him that it wasn't too serious a delusion. "A lot you know," moaned the man. "I happen to be Jewish."

Morris came home from work early one day and found his wife in bed. She said she wasn't feeling well. He went to the closet to hang up his hat and coat and to his surprise, he found a man hiding in the closet. He looked at him and shouted, "What are you doing in my closet?"
The man shrugged, "Everybody has to be somewhere."

1st Partner: "I don't like the new book-keeper you hired. She limps and stutters."
2nd Partner: "What of it?"
1st Partner: "Why did you hire her?"
2nd Partner: So she'll be easy to identify if she steals."

Little Max came home from school with terrible report cards. When reprimanded by his parents he explained to them that he was sure that his teacher was anti-Semitic. His parents thought it over and decided that they would convert rather than have their child faced with this problem throughout his life. They converted and the next report card came in even worse than the one before. They called Max in to ask him to explain. He said, "You know those Jewish kids learn faster than us gentiles."

A little old lady sat on a park bench in the Bronx. A neighbor admired her two little grandchildren and asked their ages.
The little old lady said, "The lawyer is four and the doctor is six."

She: After we're married I'll share all your troubles and sorrows.
He: But I have no troubles and sorrows.
She: Well, you will after we're married.

How was the Grand Canyon formed? A Jew dropped his penny in the sand.

"I chased an ambulance three miles."
"Did you catch it?"
"Yes, but there was already another lawyer in it."

Pincus took his religion seriously. He obeyed the Sabbath, not riding, smoking, or handling money. This particular Saturday, vacationing at a resort, he put on his red sport jacket and decided to walk through the fields. A bull, seeing the red jacket, ran after him and in a second impaled Pincus on his horns and was running wild with him. Pincus yelled. Another hiker heard it and cried: "What's the matter, Pincus?"
"I'm riding on Shabbes—help! Help!"

The first ship of the Israeli line to be launched was known as the S.S. Mein Kindt.

The man selling hot dogs on the boardwalk at Far Rockaway was shouting, "I don't care where you go or what you pay, you can't get better."
"That's right, you can't," said an oldtimer sitting on a bench. "I ate one last week and I'm not better yet."

The rabbi and the priest were having a friendly discussion. "Tell me the truth, rabbi," the priest nudged him, "have you ever committed a sin against your faith?" The rabbi thought it over. "Well," he admitted, "once a long time ago, before I became a rabbi, I ate a piece of pork."
The two sat in silence. Then, "Have you ever sinned, Father?" asked the rabbi.
The priest grinned. "Before becoming a priest, I had an affair with a woman."
More silence. Then, "Sure beats pork," said the rabbi.

He told the waiter he didn't like the looks of the codfish and the waiter said, "If it's looks you want, why don't you order goldfish?"

Jewish husbands! If you want to lose weight, here's a great new diet for you. Only eat when your wife cooks!

The movie was a touching story of the hardships of the average family during the French Revolution. But one young matron from Great Neck was unimpressed. She said to her escort, "If they were so poor, how could they afford all that antique furniture?"

"Do you know that the Mayor of Dublin is Jewish?"
"Is that so? Only in America could this happen!"

Said the tall blond Westerner to the little Jewish hooker: "$100! You really know how to hurt a goy!"

If you enjoyed this book, you will want the others
in this series;

Poems For The John

Jokes For The John

MORE Jokes For The John

Guest Register For The John

Limericks For The John

Jokes For The Head

Flushed